SINGING COWBOY STARS

SINGING COWBOY STARS

Robert W. Phillips

GIBBS·SMITH
PUBLISHER

SALT LAKE CITY

01 00 99 98 5 4 3 2

Published by Gibbs Smith, Publisher
P .O . Box 667
Layton, Utah 84041

Design by J. Scott Knudsen, Park City, Utah
Production by Scott Van Kampen

Front cover photographs: Roy Rogers and Gene Autry
from Dell comic books, Phillips Archives.

Back cover photographs: Pasty Montana from
Phillips Archives, courtesy Pasty Montana and
Bruce Fischer; Dale Evans, Rex Allen, Tex Ritter
and John Wayne from Phillips Archives.

Printed in Hong Kong

Library of Congress Cataloging-in-Publication Data

Phillips, Robert W.,1994-
Singing cowboy stars / by Robert W. Phillips
p. cm.
ISBN 0-87905-593-6 (hb)
1. Western films-History and criticism.
2. Motion picture actors and actresses-United States-Biography.
3. Country musicians-United States-Biography. I. Title
PN1995.9.W4P48 1994
791.43'6278-dc20
93-42655 CIP

o my

grandfather Joe Biggers (1887-1961),

who, in the late 1940s, fired all of my interest

in these high-riding heroes and in whose

memory I will always work.

And to my wife, Cece, and children, Scarlett,

Marty, Robert, Hank, and Michael.

CONTENTS

ACKNOWLEDGMENTS

I wish to thank all of those who share a great deal of interest in cowboy heroes, and who opened up their own memorabilia collections and shared their recollections of what it was like to live in such a golden era. They are friends of a very special kind, with whom I've shared many fond memories:

Merv Bendewald, Jerry Sienco, Jerry Gallagher, Glenn White, Ben Cunningham, Elvin Sweeten, Bob Hansen, Norman Michaels, the late Kathrine Smith, Walter Williams, Professor Ray White, Fred Rewkowski, the late Keith Kolby, Joe Knight, Jane Miller, Larry Cisewski, Jerry Carbone, and Nancy Horsley.

Heartfelt thanks to the following:

My wife, Cece, who has understood and respected my obsession with these riders of the plains and encouraged my work in documenting the excitement associated with the greatest role models this country has ever produced.

My parents, Pat and JoLain Probst, who have been a constant source of encouragement.

My brother Barry Jones, who used to help me keep our backyard "Wild West" free of "varmints and owlhoots."

My sister-in-law Susan Wisdom and son-in-law Bruce Fischer, and many nieces and nephews, who have been among my best supporters.

Patsy Montana, a real trooper who came through gloriously in the final days of photo selection.

Len Morris with Galen Productions, who provided me with my first film credit as research consultant.

The fine folks at the Gene Autry Western Heritage Museum, Los Angeles.

Phil Levine, who drove two hundred miles to fill a special request.

Dr. Charles R. Townsend, author of *San Antonio Rose: The Life and Music of Bob Wills*, who taught me through his writing the value of thorough research.

Lee Ann Rewkowski for all her computer knowledge.

To everyone in Greenpoint, Brooklyn, who treated me as if I were some sort of cowboy hero riding back from the sunset.

Jerry Ohlinger and his crew; Rhonda Lemons at Empire Publishing; Paul and Gayla at Film Favorites; Bob Gallagher; and Ken Galente at Silver Screen Photo for producing several hard-to-find photos.

Bob King, Norman Kietzer, Helen Houser, Kathy Streten, Tanya Lane, Julie Semrau, Victoria Kramer, John Koenig, Barbara Jacksier, Brian Galligan, Jackie Carnegie, William Jacobson, Frances Graham, Judy Wilson, Boyd Magers, Katrina Kelly, and Bill Black for keeping my name on the newsstands and in people's homes, helping me to spread the gospel of the values and ideals connected with our cowboy heroes.

Steve Laird and Sherry Lynn Confer for making all the research possible.

My publisher, Gibbs Smith, for helping our vision become a reality, and for saturating the country with my books and poster sets on the essential cowboy hero.

A very special sort of thanks to the staff at Gibbs Smith, Publisher—my editors who have made this and the previous projects much more than enjoyable; they have the ability to turn work into absolute fun: Lynda Sessions, Gail Yngve, Tom Smart, and Madge Baird. ☐

INTRODUCTION

Singing cowboys of the 1930s to 1950s were an unmatched bunch, and together a couple of dozen of them are responsible for a worldwide fascination that is still present today for anyone and everything western. The singing cowboys rode across the silver screen every Saturday afternoon at the local picture show, transporting the Wild West into America's cities and towns and taming it before our very eyes. We loved to imagine ourselves riding alongside them in ten-gallon hats, packing a pair of six-guns on our hips, and wearing fringed shirt, silver spurs, maybe picking on a Gibson guitar.

Now, wait just a durn minute! A guitar? That's the way it was, all right. The hero would ride off into the sunset either with or without the maiden. Either way, it was always his choice; for while saving the ranch from the villains, he'd somehow found the time to pause, get out his guitar, and win her heart. These guys always found the time for a song, even while running rustlers into the hills.

Many city dwellers got their first notion of the cowboy life from these fellows, and rural folks had their horizons expanded. They taught us all some songs we'll never forget: "I've Got Spurs That Jingle, Jangle, Jingle," or "Back in the Saddle Again." For as long as America has been fascinated with the image of the cowboy, it has had a love affair with the songs of the cowboy.

The beginnings of the phenomenon can be seen in Nathan Howard Thorpe's 1908 publication of *Songs of the Cowboy*. In 1915 Curley Fletcher wrote the timeless poem "The Strawberry Roan." Concert singer Bently Hall made recordings of "The Dying Cowboy" and "Jesse James" at the very beginning of the commercial recording industry. Carl Sprague's 1925 recordings included cowboy songs such as "When the Work's All Done This Fall."

Texas cowhand Jules Verne Allen performed songs such as "Longhorn Luke" over the radio,

telling of a life he knew firsthand. The phenomenon kept growing with Goebel Reeves's recording of "The Cowboy Prayer." Then there were Harry McClintock's performance of "Sam Bass," Otto Gray touring radio stations between 1928 and 1932, and John White introducing the songs of the American cowboy to a New York audience.

Interest in cowboy songs really took off in the 1930s, when they were worked into the medium of the B-western film. Cowboy star Ken Maynard gets the credit for coming up with the idea. From the advent of the sound film, cowboy stars spent two years trying to get used to working with dialogue, and most simply couldn't cut it. In 1930 Maynard explored a new way to use the medium when he introduced a singing trio in his film *The Fighting*

Legion. The next year, Warner Baxter, playing the role of the Cisco Kid, took time out to serenade the beautiful Conchita Montenegro.

In 1933 Maynard returned as a fiddler and ventriloquist in *The Fiddlin' Buckaroo*. He also starred in *The Strawberry Roan*, which featured the well-known song of the same name. Also, in 1933 budding star John Wayne reluctantly got into the act as "Singing Sandy" in the film *Riders of Destiny*. Still, it took another year and another event for the singing cowboy idea to really catch on. That event was the arrival in Hollywood of radio singer Gene Autry, who first appeared in Ken Maynard's 1934 film *In Old Santa Fe*. Maynard's talents ran more to roping and riding, and Gene simply took on a role that Maynard couldn't sustain. He went on to make his starring debut in the strange western/science fiction serial *Phantom Empire*, and this became the film that gave definitive birth to the singing cowboy phenomenon. Through what critic John Tuska called the "Autry Phantasy," Gene was able to overcome any danger, no matter how grave, with little more than a guitar and a song.

After *Phantom Empire* came Autry' first starring serial film, the hugely successful *Tumblin' Tumbleweeds*, featuring the classic song of the same name. His voice and style made him number one and set the standard for other singing cowboys. Countless aspirants competed against Autry. Dick Foran made his debut just a couple of months after the release of *Tumblin' Tumbleweeds*, and the string of new stars continued for more than twenty years—all the way up to cowboy-great Rex Allen in the mid-fifties and beyond.

Gene Autry single-handedly gave birth to a stereotype that has seen no end, extending beyond the music market to toys, comics, and even fashion. Roy Rogers was close on his boot heels and deserves as much credit as Autry for keeping the wheels in motion. Guitars, cap guns, and other paraphernalia branded with the likenesses of Gene and Roy became big sellers. Complete cowboy outfits offered through the Sears and Roebuck catalogs started a fashion trend.

The stereotype, image, and legend, is of a cowboy as quick with his guitar as with his six-guns, a man who can right all wrongs no matter what trouble he encounters and celebrate the event with a song. The singing cowboy has become an institution. He is the ultimate embodiment of an American ideal: the simple, hard-working cowpuncher as a moral hero. After all, bad guys don't sing.

Today, the impact is still felt and the legend lives on. At western film festivals and other cowboy gatherings, it's fairly common to see real live singing cowboys. Decked out in Stetsons or custom-made hats, wearing vests, bandanas, with pants tucked inside their boots, they strum a guitar and sing from a seemingly endless repertoire.

The rest of the singing cowboy story can be found in the pages of this book. These are tales of the men and women behind a uniquely American icon. They are the singing cowboys and cowgirls who have earned a special place in the continuing saga of the West. ☐

KEN MAYNARD

Ken Maynard was the first cowboy star to use musical interludes in films. He even took part in the singing on occasion—and he was impressed. His studio was not. From the 1920s to the 1940s, he ranked high on the list of box-office favorites. But he was better suited to cleaning up the wild and woolly West with fists, fancy riding, and six-guns than he ever was with a song and instrument.

The son of a carpenter, Ken was born in Vevay, Indiana, in 1895, one of five children. Spending his childhood in Kentucky and Indiana, Ken ran off at the ripe old

In this publicity still, Ken Maynard doesn't look like an hombre who could burst into song. Phillips Archives.

age of fourteen to join a medicine show. He was sent back home, but his parents gave him permission to join a traveling circus at sixteen.

Maynard worked with carnivals, Wild West shows, and circuses. He used this time to perfect skills he would eventually use as a cowboy hero on the Hollywood back lots—trick riding and fancy roping. After army duty during World War I, Ken returned to circus work and ventured into the rodeo arena. In 1920 he won the astounding sum of $42,000 in Oregon as the Pendleton Rodeo All-Around Champion Cowboy.

Ken traveled to Los Angeles with the Ringling Brothers and Barnum and Bailey Circus Wild West Show. There he met western box-office hero Buck Jones, who encouraged him to take a shot at Hollywood. He took the advice and hit the target with a contract at Fox Studios. Within several years, he had ridden to the front of the pack for

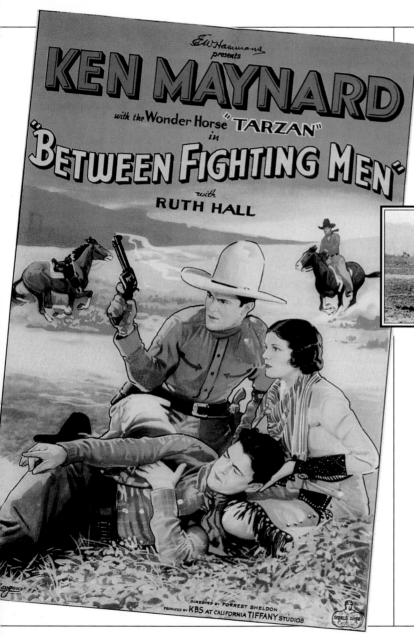

DIRECTED BY FORREST SHELDON
PRODUCED BY KBS AT CALIFORNIA TIFFANY STUDIOS

the cowboy shoot-'em-up fans of the period.

By the time he signed with First National, Ken and his horse, Tarzan, had quite a following. His death-defying stunt work gave the other cowboy stars some fierce competition. His handsome features and horsemanship more than made up for whatever acting skills he lacked.

Maynard moved to Universal Films, where he made eight pictures and took advantage of a new concept, musical soundtracks and music. Proficient on several instruments, Ken recorded two songs for

Columbia Records, "The Lone Star Trail" and "The Cowboy's Lament." On film he was the first of the box-office buckaroos to exercise his vocal chords in song. His real break came with the advent of sound in 1928. He burst into song on two occasions in the 1930 film *Sons of the Saddle*, backed by three other cowpokes. The cowboy songs on film were called "Trail Herd Song" and "Down the Home Trail With You." Ken's singing came off as amateurish, but the rough edges seemed to lend an air of authenticity to his performances.

In 1931 and 1932 Ken worked at Tiffany and World Wide Studios where he stuck to his riding and roping, but he found his way back to Universal in 1933, playing his fiddle in the aptly titled *Fiddlin' Buckaroo*. In *The Trail Drive* he sat beside a campfire, looking the part of the authentic cowboy performing on his banjo. Next, the hero and his saddle-mates sang "Strawberry Roan" in the 1933 film of the same name. He even wrote the music for the title song of his film *Wheels of Destiny*.

In 1934 Maynard changed studio homes again, moving this time to Mascot Pictures. The film *In Old Santa Fe* started off with one of Maynard's own songs, but the head

Although Maynard is listed among singing cowboys, he is best known for daring movie stunts performed on Tarzan. Phillips Archives.

of Mascot, Nat Levine, had little appreciation for Ken's singing ability, and so his voice was dubbed. Millions of fans who now remember Gene as the first of the great singing cowboy legends are indebted to Maynard, a pioneer of the horse opera who originally created the audience that would propel Gene and numerous others to fame.

After making more than fifty sound movies, Maynard left film

work in 1940 to hit the rodeo circuit once again. He returned to Hollywood in 1943 for *The Trail Blazers* series. Then, after two years, Ken retired from film and continued to make appearances at rodeos and state fairs. Following the death of his wife, he became a recluse, dying at age seventy-seven, living broke in a trailer, after suffering from alcoholism and malnutrition. □

JOHN WAYNE

JOHN WAYNE AND THE SAGA OF SINGIN' SANDY

O f all film stars, John Wayne was the ultimate version of the American cowboy. From the great classic *Stagecoach* through the equally great *True Grit* and beyond, The Duke portrayed the great American hero before audiences around the world. For showing uncompromised morals and undaunted patriotism through dozens of westerns and war epics, a Congressional Medal was struck in his honor.

Though John Wayne is not known as a singing cowboy, he appeared as "Singin' Sandy" in a series of films for Monogram. Many still claim that Wayne's voice was dubbed with the voice of Smith Ballew. Phillips Archives.

So why is John Wayne included in a book about singing cowboys? Though we may never understand the exact nature of Wayne's contribution to this subgenre of the western, the significance is that, regardless of whether he was actually doing the voicing or not, he was one of the first to portray the singing cowboy on film.

In 1930 film studios began experimenting with musical cowboy films for a couple of years. In 1933 Paul Malvern, a producer at Lone Star Productions, had the idea of turning John Wayne into a singing cowboy. Wayne agreed to the job, having just completed his contract at Warner Brothers, but he was actually worried that his career might suffer if he became typecast as a cowboy. There was no question about the quality of his acting, but The Duke didn't exactly pass his singing test, and he had no idea how to play the guitar. Undeterred, the producers decided they could dub the voice and guitar

with a real singer and real musician;
all Wayne would have to do was
move his lips and pretend to strum
away. *Riders of Destiny* went into
production and Wayne became
"Singin' Sandy" Saunders, an
undercover G-man.

After the release of *Riders of
Destiny,* the Lone Star series continued for a total of sixteen films.
To John Wayne, the idea of singing
cowboys was a little sissified. He
simply could not fathom himself in
the role. He was later quoted by his
wife, Pilar, as saying that he felt
like a "!#@! pansy." By the time
this series ended, Gene Autry had
come riding along, and Hollywood
had its singing cowboy star.

Though some film historians have
credited Smith Ballew for the vocals
in the "Singin' Sandy" films, numerous others dispute this theory, and
some hold that it *is* Big John.
Though it is unclear how the controversy got started, it has lasted many
years. Regardless, John Wayne left
an unmistakable mark on the world
of the singing cowboy. □

GENE AUTRY

"Cowboy" was just a way of life for a boy growing up in the far North Texas town of Tioga. Born September 29, 1907, Orvon Gene Autry learned to ride just as soon as he got big enough. By age five he had learned how to sing from his Baptist-preacher grandad, and later, using eight dollars he'd saved baling hay on his uncle's farm, Gene bought his first guitar from the Sears and Roebuck catalog. Little could he have imagined that this small wooden instrument would start him down a path that would eventually earn him millions.

As a teenager, Gene moved across

The handsome young Gene Autry, found lasting popularity with western film fans. (Courtesy Gene Autry)

western movie hits

1953 edition

special features:

BEST WESTERN OF THE YEAR:
pack train (gene autry) 3-11
BOY ROGERS' TV ALBUM:

20 FULL-LENGTH STORIES

1953

Gene Autry

in

PACK TRAIN

Best Western of the Year

the best western of the year
GENE AUTRY'S
"PACK TRAIN"

the Red River into Oklahoma, where he picked up experience performing in school and on local stages, often accompanied on the piano by his cousin Louise. His first big exposure came when he joined the Fields Brothers Marvelous Medicine Show for three months at fifteen dollars a week.

He later found more stable employment with the railroad. One lonesome night in 1927, while working the telegraph at the Chelsea, Oklahoma station, Gene was passing the time with his guitar when a stranger dropped by. He handed over a telegram for Gene to send, said he was impressed with his singing, and offered some advice: "With some hard work, young man, you might have something. You ought to go to New York and get yourself a job on the radio."

The stranger turned out to be

In the 1940s and 1950s, Gene Autry's image graced the cover of many film-related magazines. Above, from the movie *Pack Train*, Gene with Kenne Duncan.

COLUMBIA PICTURES presents

GENE AUTRY
World's Greatest Cowboy
and **CHAMPION**
World's Wonder Horse

SONS OF NEW MEXICO

with
Gail **DAVIS** · Robert **ARMSTRONG** · Dick **JONES** · Frankie **DARRO**

Written by PAUL GANGELIN
Directed by JOHN ENGLISH · Produced by ARMAND SCHAEFER
A GENE AUTRY PRODUCTION

humorist and country philosopher Will Rogers. Gene took the man's advice, trying his luck in New York a year later. As it turned out, the big city wasn't ready for a singing cowboy just yet, but Gene had acquired the itch for show business. He returned to Tulsa and landed a job as "Oklahoma's Yodelin' Cowboy" on KVOO Radio, with the backup of Jimmy Wilson's Catfish String Band. His show gained an appreciable audience, and he used it to plug numerous personal appearances over the air, performing in Kiwanis Clubs, schoolhouses, and private parties.

With a friend from the railroad, chief night dispatcher Jimmy Long, Gene penned a song called "That Silver-Haired Daddy of Mine" and sang it over KVOO. The listeners were delighted with it. Gene was given a glowing write-up in *The Tulsa World* and found the confidence to tackle the big city once again. On October 9, 1929, he cut his first sides for Victor Records in New York City, "My Dreaming of You" and

Front-row kids used to stand and gaze at the movie posters under glass on the outside walls of the theater buildings. On Saturday afternoons, sometimes the lines for the westerns would extend for blocks. (Poster left and photo right courtesy Gene Autry)

"My Alabama Home." Art Satherley was also interested in Gene, and the now-legendary head of ARC (later known as Columbia Records) promised to make him "number one." Gene recorded six more sides for three hundred dollars, which was an awful lot of money in 1929.

Gene had a banner year in 1932; he took Jimmy Long's niece, Ina Mae Spivey, for his bride and waxed the Autry/Long hit "That Silver-Haired Daddy of Mine." The recording quickly sold a million copies, became the first Gold Record ever awarded, and was eventually picked up by scores of other singers.

Sales of ARC records through the Sears and Roebuck mail-order catalog assured great exposure for Gene throughout rural America, and he became a popular regular on the "National Barn Dance" radio broadcast. Still, Gene had even higher goals than records and radio. He began writing letters to Nat Levine, the president of Mascot Pictures.

His timing couldn't have been better. Hollywood had been experimenting with musical interludes in Western films for a while, and Levine had the idea of creating an entire musical western featuring a singing cowboy. Gene signed with Mascot in 1934, landing a guest spot singing two songs in a barnyard dance sequence in the Ken Maynard film *In Old Santa Fe*. Gene's first starring part came in the twelve-chapter serial *The Phantom Empire*, in the role of a radio entertainer out on a dude ranch who discovers an underground kingdom. Complete with flame throwers and ray guns, the

Smiley Burnette as "Frog Millhouse" could literally steal the show from cowboy star Gene Autry with his zany antics.

film was an unusual combination of western action and science fiction that had been inspired by the discovery of Carlsbad Caverns.

The serial was successful, and Gene was signed to play the starring role in *Tumbling Tumbleweeds*. Riding alongside Gene was Smiley Burnette, a "round mound of sound" with the self-taught ability to play countless instruments. Smiley had started out in show business as a one-man band in vaudeville, and met Gene while working at a tiny, 100-watt radio station in Tuscola, Illinois. Gene and Smiley eventually

Millions of record players wore out millions of Gene Autry records through the 1940s and '50s. This is a ten-inch L.P. that included such classic recordings as "Back in the Saddle Again."

made sixty-two films together.

Tumbling Tumbleweeds became a smash hit, and before long Gene became "America's Favorite Cowboy," reigning supreme from 1937 to 1955 astride his magnificent horse Champion. He became the first western-film star to headline the world-famous Madison Square Garden Championship Rodeo, and in a 1939 tour that took him to Ireland drew a crowd of 750,000 admirers in Dublin.

When World War II broke out, Gene traded his saddle for an airplane seat, serving as a sergeant in the Air Transport Command of the U.S. Air Corps. Between flights he made a number of recordings for the War Department, including "There's a Star-Spangled Banner Waving Somewhere," and also managed to release a few songs through Columbia in 1944 and 1945.

After the war, Gene returned to the movies, filming *Sioux City Sue* and four additional films for Republic and then moving to Columbia, forming his own production company. As his own boss, Gene was able to take advantage of increased budgets and even do some color outings. Films

such as *Strawberry Roan* (1948) and *Pack Train* (1953) did well.

With eighty-nine feature westerns under his belt, Gene entered the up-and-coming television market with a show turned out by his own company, Flying A Productions. "The Gene Autry Show" featured Gene and saddle pard Pat Buttram bringing justice wherever in the West it was needed, taking time out only to sing a song or make a friend. Introduced by the classic theme song "Back in the Saddle Again," the series saw ninety-one episodes broadcast over CBS through 1956.

Beyond film and television, Gene's show-business career saw hundreds of published songs and 635 recordings, including classics for adults ("Back in the Saddle Again," "Mexicali Rose," "South of the Border," "You Are My Sunshine") and for children ("Rudolph the Red-Nosed Reindeer," "Peter Cottontail," "Frosty the Snowman," "Here Comes Santa Claus"). A successful radio show, "Melody Ranch," aired from 1940 until 1956. There were books, toys, and comics tying in with the good-guy, singing-cowboy image he helped to create. Gene also owned ranches, raised stock for rodeos, and for years toured with his own rodeo.

He didn't need to be peeled out

of the saddle when the time for singing cowboys passed. According to Gene, in the finest Old West tradition, he just "changed horses" in the mid-1960s, becoming a millionaire through his interests in real estate, film and TV production, broadcast media, and sports.

Gene Autry is the only entertainer with five stars on the Hollywood Walk of Fame, for his work on radio, records, movies, television and live theatrical and rodeo appearances. He was the only star voted as high as number four in box-office drawing power by the Exhibitors of America by 1940 (after Mickey Rooney, Spencer Tracy and Clark Gable) in addition to being number one in the annual poll of western stars. His only serious rival was Roy Rogers, who came to the fore while Gene was in World War II from 1942–

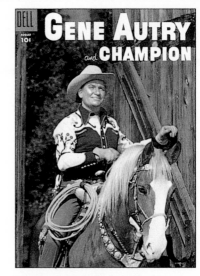

Gene Autry and Champion galloped through the pages of a comic book series from 1941–59. More than 120 issues were published

1946. Postwar polls showed them equal as the top singing cowboys.

Gene Autry has received a lifetime of honors. He was elected to the Country Music Hall of Fame in 1969 and named to the Cowboy Hall of Fame of Great Westerners in 1980. He founded the Gene Autry Museum in Los Angeles, which houses one of the world's greatest collections of Western relics and papers. His saddle pal Pat Buttram once said of Autry, "Gene used to ride off into the sunset. Now he owns it." □

$\mathcal{D}$ICK FORAN

ohn Nicholas Foran was
born on June 18, 1910 or
1911, in Flemington,
New Jersey. As a young
man he studied at
Princeton to become a geolo-
gist. After leaving college,
Foran sought adventure
through such jobs as seaman
and investigator with the
Pennsylvania Railroad. But the
prospect of a glamorous singing
career in Hollywood seemed far
more exciting to him.

His acting experience began
with summer-stock productions
under the stage name Nick Foran.
His film debut came in 1934, with
Gentlemen Are Born. In 1935, after
appearing in the musical *Stand Up
and Cheer* with Warner Baxter and
Shirley Temple, he rode onto the
musical range as Dick Foran atop
his palomino Smoke, with Warner

**Singing Cowboy Dick Foran leans
on a handsome silver-mounted Ed Bohlin-
style saddle in this publicity still.
Phillips Archives.**

Brothers issuing the paychecks.
Moonlight on the Prairie was his
first singing western.

Unlike some others in his
field, Dick Foran never stum-
bled because of his opera
training. His audiences
accepted him since he came
across as a natural cowboy
singer and had great personality and charm as well. He was
tall, clean-cut and handsome
and could handle a song with
the best of them.

It is our loss that Foran was
reduced to mostly supporting-actor
roles after having been on the list of
top money-making western stars
from 1936 through 1938. He rose to
the number-four position in 1937.
Foran's dozen singing cowboy feature westerns for Warner Brothers
included *Song of the Saddle* (1936),
Guns of the Pecos (1937), *Empty*

Foran is pinned down in this action still from his 1937 Warner Brothers film *Guns of the Pecos*. Phillips Archives

Holsters (1937), and *Cowboy From Brooklyn* (1937).

In 1938 he hitched his horse at Universal Studios. They used him in every kind of outing imaginable, from horror films to dramatic roles to comedies. His westerns for Universal included starring roles in two serials—"Winners of the West" (1940) and "Riders of Death Valley" (1941)—and supporting roles in numerous other films. In the early 1950s he captured dramatic roles on television, appearing in such shows as "Kraft Mystery Theater."

By the time of his last film appearance in 1967, Foran had been in over two hundred pictures. □

 RT DAVIS

Audrey "Art" Davis first saw light of day in Paradise, one of those blink-and-you'll-miss-it towns in the north-western part of Texas. He wasn't long in Paradise, though. When he was about two, his family loaded up all they had and started moving, first to a tiny town in the Oklahoma hills, then to the northeast Texas town Lewisville. Art learned early about hard work: busting up peanuts, picking cotton, and plowing ground. His father played fiddle, banjo, and guitar, so music was a big part of the lad's early life. By the time he was seven he had become an accomplished fiddler. At age nine, he was taking formal lessons for the fee of $1.00 each.

Art's parents divorced, and his brother Jay and he went with their dad. They wound up living in the

Photo from the back cover of _Art's Music Memories._ Courtesy/copyright A&L Productions.

heart of Dallas, where Art enrolled at the Technical High School. Th[e] young lad had a calling for sport[s] and a passion for music, lettering i[n] football and playing clarinet in th[e] school band. It was at the hig[h] school that he first played with fe[l]lows like Jim Boyd (the brother [of] Bill "Cowboy Rambler" Boyd[)], musicians who would one day carv[e] their names in Texas music history[.]

Horsemanship was as importan[t] as the music for any real cowbo[y] musician. Art gained some ridin[g] experience when he and his brothe[r] joined up with the 112th Cavalry [of] the Texas National Guard. He eve[n] saw a little action when his outfi[t] was sent to Sherman, Texas, t[o] quell a race riot and ease the ten[-] sions following a lynching there[.] His education in the saddle contin[-] ued through a stint at Cam[p] Walters, Texas.

AD-1981

ART'S
MUSIC
MEMORIES

Art Davis

Art thought of getting a more steady career as a lawyer, but his try at law school didn't take, and he soon returned to music.

Art Davis teamed up with some of the musicians from his early days to record *Art's Music Memories,* **released in 1981. Courtesy/Copyright A&L Productions.**

In the early 1930s Art was playing for money wherever he could find an audience. Jim Boyd and he organized The Rhythm Aces and also managed to get in with some popular regional bands including Milton Brown and his Musical Brownies, Roy Newman and his Boys, The Light Crust Doughboys, and Bill Boyd's Cowboy Ramblers. All of these groups played the hot Texas fiddle music that local folks loved to dance to, music that evolved into Western Swing.

In 1934 with the Cowboy Ramblers, Art was recording songs for the RCA subsidiary Bluebird Records—such tunes as "I'm Gonna Hop Off the Train," "Going Back to My Texas Home," "Barn Dance Rag," "I Can't Tame Wild Women," and the now classic "Way Out There." In those days Art did his running around in a Model A Ford, complete with rumble seat. Foot loose and fancy free with nothing or anyone to hold him down, he worked when he pleased, playing dances, performing on radio and working recording sessions. A master of the fiddle, clarinet, and mandolin, Art had no trouble finding a job or a good time.

While a staff musician at Dallas's WRR Radio, Art's biggest break came from the new Hollywood sensation Gene Autry, who rode into town in need of a back-up fiddler for a recording session. On September 22, 1935, with Art as his fiddler, he put to wax "Be Nobody's Darling But Mine" for the ARC group later known as Columbia Records.

Gene was taken with Art's work and offered him jobs in his movies and on road tours. Art hung in with Gene during the three years that Autry was beginning to establish himself as the country's number-one singing cowboy, appearing in about twenty-five pictures as well as backing him on one-nighters and week-long stands. Eventually he met up with a certain screenwriter who talked him into signing for Equity Pictures' *Adventures of the Masked Phantom*. He received third billing under the name Larry Mason, behind Monte Rawlins and Sonny Lamont, but the contract he signed prevented him from working on any film not directed by the screenwriter, and he lost out on work as a result. He ended up heading back to the Southwest in frustration, knowing he could stay busy there playing dances while waiting for the contract to expire. As soon as it did, he headed out West again, and landed second billing in a Tim McCoy feature in 1941 and with Lee Powell and his old Texas buddy Bill Boyd cranked out six serial westerns from late 1941 through early 1942. As musical westerns were the thing at the time, Art did pretty well, commanding a larger fee than either of his costars.

Art went on a War Bond Drive with cowboy film star Roy Rogers, then joined the U. S. Navy. The Armed Forces didn't cramp his music or style as he put together a band in Florida that played for officers' dances.

Following a discharge September 1945, Art headed back to Tulsa, where he landed a radio program and toured with a new band. He and his Rhythm Riders appeared in a musical short, filmed in Dallas and released by Astor Films, *A Cowboy's Holiday*. It marked Art's final appearance before the cameras.

Even in the 1980s Art was still earning a living with music, recording an album of *Art's Music Memories* with legendary Texas musicians Jim Boyd and Marvin Montgomery. Once one of that elite Hollywood group known as the singing cowboys, Art Davis never gave up performing for admirers of a western song or a fine fiddle tune. □

FRED SCOTT

In this pose Scott seems to be about to ride off into the sunset in search of adventure. Phillips Archives.

Born in Fresno, California, on February 14, 1902, Fred Lee Scott didn't have to make the usual aspiring star's trek across the country to get where the action was. The son of a bricklayer and a mother who could well remember the covered-wagon days, Fred studied voice as a child. His entrance into show business came at age sixteen, when he landed a role as a detective for the Fresno Community Players. He later worked in a musical for a traveling troupe with the Kermess Company and sang a concert for the Pro Music Society in Fresno.

When Fred's family moved to Llano del Rio in California's Mojave

SPECTRUM PICTURES CORP. *presents*

FRED SCOTT *and* MARION SHILLING *in* "ROMANCE RIDES THE RANGE"

Romance Rides the Range, 1936, was Scott's first starring role. Phillips Archives.

Desert region, he got his first taste of real cowboy life. He found employment on a cattle ranch, riding horses and rounding up cattle. He tried to get film roles on horseback but was unsuccessful. In the early twenties Fred finally landed parts in silent films, and then for three years he was Helen Twelvetree's leading man at Pathe. When he finally made it into his first western, he was given a singing part in a Harry Carey film.

Fred left film work for a while and went into opera and stage performances. He sang at the famous Biltmore Bowl in Los Angeles, performing mostly cowboy songs. It turned out to be an important job, for while appearing he met and married a dancer with George White's Scandals and was also discovered by producer Jed Buel.

After years of sometimes unlikely preparation, Fred found his place on the Hollywood range at last. He made several series oaters for Spectrum Pictures, films like *Romance Rides the Range* (1936), *Melody of the Plains* (1937), *The Roaming Cowboy* (1937), *Song and Bullets* (1938), *In Old Montana* (1939), *Two-Gun Troubador* (1939), *Ridin' the Trail* (1940), and *Rodeo Rhythm* (1942).

Fred was the first of the singing cowboys to have had opera training. He sang his way across the celluloid prairie with a set of pipes that got him billed as "The Silvery-Voiced Baritone," then, more in tune with the cowboy theme, "The Silvery-Voiced Buckaroo."

With his horse White Dust, Fred made nearly two dozen films, getting great comic relief from side-kicks such as Al St. John. One of Fred's producers was the phenomenal comedian Stan Laurel of Laurel and Hardy fame. As if the music, comedy, and action weren't enough, Fred also did a fair amount of his own stunt work, including the horseback tricks known as the "pony express" and the "crouper mount."

After retiring from film in the late 1940s, Fred worked in real estate, eventually settling down to manage his own rental properties. Physical conditioning and mental acuity were always high priorities for him, and he maintained lifelong interests in swimming, linguistics, and music. He finally passed away in 1991, leaving his fans with memories of a cowboy star who combined it all: horsemanship, charisma, comedy, and one of the best-trained voices ever heard as a Hollywood buckaroo. □

Two-gun troubadour Fred Scott is all smiles in this publicity still. Phillips Archives.

$\mathcal{T}$EX RITTER

Tex looks as though he's in the mood for no tomfoolery.
Phillips Archives.

Woodward Maurice Ritter came in to the role of singing cowboy naturally by absorbing the traditions that surrounded him in the East Texas town Murvaul, where he was born January 12, 1905. The drawl and the mannerisms were passed down from his father, a farmer and cowboy. The music was a part of life in church, in the community, and at home.

Tex attended a one-room school that doubled as a church on Sundays. It was so close to the Ritter home that schoolteachers often lived with the family.

Old-time singing schools were common in East Texas, and traveling singing teachers would often pass through town. The family sang at home as well, mostly church songs. Of the three boys in the fam-

ily, Tex was considered to have the least ability to carry a tune, but with music all around him, the notes finally stuck. As he got older, he developed a penchant for the traditional cowboy songs.

The young Ritter left the area to attend the University of Texas law school for five years. There, he met the much-acclaimed J. Frank Dobie, an English professor, writer, and western folklorist. This association fanned the fires of Tex's enthusiasm for western song and folklore.

He also attended Northwestern University in Chicago, and Tex might have been a law-school graduate if hard times on the horizon had not changed his plans. When the Great Depression hit, most people were happy to find work at all. Tex ventured to Houston, Texas, where he sang on KPRC Radio in 1929 and also performed one-nighters across

PRC Pictures presents

TEX **RITTER**
Dave **O'BRIEN**
AS **THE TEXAS RANGERS**

THE WHISPERING SKULL

with **GUY WILKERSON**   Screenplay by HARRY FRASER   Directed by ELMER CLIFTON   Produced by ARTHUR ALEXANDER

the South and Midwest. He tried to sell life insurance and considered jobs for oil companies, but none of them was what he really wanted.

Then, in 1930, Tex learned that a western show was being produced for the Broadway stage by Theater

Tex teamed up with Dave O'Brien and Guy Wilkerson to continue *The Texas Rangers* trio, an eight-part series for PRC. Phillips Archives.

Though straight-shootin', Tex seems to have the odds against him in this movie still. Phillips Archives.

Guild. His thick Texas drawl, which had hurt his chances for commercial appeal until then, helped him win a job in the show. Tex understudied the part of Franchot Tone, played a cowboy, and sang four songs in the play *Green Grow the Lilacs*, which would become famous ten years later as *Oklahoma*. The play officially marked the start of Ritter's singing-cowboy career.

After a brief interval at home, Tex returned to New York and got a job on WOR Radio, singing with The Lone Star Rangers on one of the first western music shows ever to be broadcast in The Big Apple. From there he went to WINS, where he appeared on a children's show called "Cowboy Tom's Roundup." Ritter and two others portrayed five characters, performing a new script each day.

Tex worked in two more plays, *The Roundup* and *Mother Lode*, and landed a recording contract with ARC that saw several releases, including "Rye Whiskey," which would always remain in his repertoire. He worked the college lecture circuit doing recitals, appeared at the Madison Square Garden Rodeo as a featured singer in 1932, and wrangled his own show, "Tex Ritter's Campfire," on WHN Radio.

Texas songbird Tex Ritter was all action in his comic book series by Fawcett/Charlton, which saw forty-six issues from 1950 to 1959. Phillips Archives.

In 1934 he became part of the WHN "Barn Dance," which he cohosted with cowboy singer Ray Whitley.

It only took a jump across the country for Tex to get into the movies. In 1936 independent producer Edward Finney figured Tex could step right into the arena. In his first outing, *Song of the Gringo*, his authentic way with a cowboy ballad helped turn him into a real star, despite the film's low budget.

Tex's contract with Finney expired in 1941, after twenty oaters for Monogram, which he considered to be his finest films as a western hero. Next, he landed at Columbia, a studio that hadn't yet latched onto a singing cowboy, where he was teamed with Bill Elliott for a string of eight westerns. In 1942 he also became one of the first artists to record for Capitol Records, a corral he stayed in for the rest of his life. He roped in other talent as well for Capitol, artists such as honky-tonk band leader Hank Thompson. Many of the songs Tex recorded were also used in his films and came to be associated with him entirely, songs such as "Jingle, Jangle, Jingle," "Jealous Heart," and "Blood on the Saddle."

After leaving Columbia, he kicked off the singing cowboy phenomenon for yet another studio, Universal Pictures, splitting credits with Johnny Mack Brown for seven sagebrush sagas. Universal eventually met with financial woes, ending Tex's employment there, but before that happened he got to ride three times as the picture's starring white-hatted hero.

Moving on to PRC, another company with a close eye on the budget, Tex became one of the studio's "Texas Rangers," riding the back lots with Dave O'Brien and Guy Wilkerson for eight more films. His film career finally came to an end in 1945, but Tex was never inclined to hang up his spurs.

He joined a touring show, riding his beautiful horse, White Flash, before large crowds. In the early 1950s composer Dimitri Tiomkin asked him to sing the song "High Noon" for the film of the same name. Both the film and the song became Oscar-winning classics. The hit was a big boost to Tex's career, and he moved on to regular television appearances on "Town Hall Party" and then his own show, "Tex Ritter's Ranch Party," seen from 1957 to 1958. He also made guest appearances on "Zane Grey Theater" and "Shotgun Slade."

Through the 1960s Tex was regarded as a living legend—hero of fifty-eight B-musical westerns; a fine singer, songwriter, and recording artist; a historian of western folklore; and, along with Roy Rogers and Gene Autry, one of the three great singing cowboys. Tex saw a big hit record with "I Dreamed of a Hillbilly Heaven." In 1964 he became the first living entertainer to be inducted into the prestigious Country Music Hall of Fame, and the Grand Ole Opry extended him a lifetime contract. He also found his way into the National Cowboy Hall of Fame and the National Songwriter's Association Hall of Fame. After he and his family moved to the country music capital Nashville, Tennessee, Tex was drafted as a Republican candidate for United States senator and eventually ran, unsuccessfully, for governor of Tennessee.

Until a heart attack ended his life on January 2, 1974, Tex Ritter continued his personal appearances, bringing delight to fans of country and western music everywhere he went. He took the life and the sound from his East Texas birthplace, refashioned them as his own, and helped spread cowboy ways from coast to coast. □

***J*ACK RANDALL**

Jack Randall on his horse, Rusty, blazed across the silver screen as the star of only five films for Monogram. Among all the notable singing cowboy stars, his career was probably the shortest.

Addison Owen Randall was born May 12, 1906, in Quincy, Illinois (or, as some sources claim, San Fernando, California). He was the son of two newspaper writers, Edgar O. and Lillian Langdon Randall, and was the brother of western film star Bob Livingston.

The family moved to California, where young Randall worked in stage pro-

Multi-talented Randall carried trigger-less six-guns that he fired by fanning the hammer. Phillips Archives.

ductions then in several RKO films, even landing a role in a vehicle for Ginger Rogers and Fred Astaire. After moving to Monogram, he won his first starring role in a 1937 shoot-'em-up.

Randall had a great voice for delivering lines, but the recording techniques used by the studios didn't do his singing voice justice. The engineers had him lip-synch his recordings, often while bouncing up and down on horseback, all the while being filmed at fairly close-up camera angles. Because of the poor recording, weak scripts, and uneven directing, his singing-cowboy career at the top of the bill lasted only from August 1937 to April 1938.

Jack was twice married to Louise Stanley, a heroine in more than a dozen western

ial called *The Royal Mounted Rides Again*. During the making of the serial, with Randall playing the part of the bad guy, his life came to an early and tragic end. On July 16, 1945, the studio skimped on stunt men to save money. In one version of the story, Jack was involved in a tug-of-war at breakneck speed, fighting a hard-headed horse who wanted to go one direction around a tree, while the cowboy had chosen another. Randall's hat took to the wind. Attempting to grab it, he lost his balance and fell from the saddle, striking the tree. Another version is that the violent fall occurred as the result of a heart attack Jack suffered during the filming of the scene. The controversy that surrounds the accident may never be resolved.

Jack Randall's starring roles included the 1937 and 1938 horse operas *Riders of the Dawn, Danger Valley, Stars Over Arizona, Where the West Begins,* and *Land of Fighting Men*. He certainly deserved more attention than his short career allowed. □

films between 1937 and 1940. After his starring work, Randall worked in several more films for Monogram—a total of twenty-two. After leaving the studio, he appeared in several non-westerns, using the name Allan Byron. By the early 1940s he was working exclusively in supporting roles.

In 1945 Universal had him ink his name on a contract that laid the groundwork for the filming of a ser-

JAMES NEWILL

James Newill was born August 12, 1911, in Pittsburgh, Pennsylvania. When a young man, he enrolled at the University of Southern California, majoring in music. James had sung opera and worked the vaudeville circuit for a while when a talent scout entered his life in 1936. The next year, Newill made his film debut in *Something To Sing About*, starring James Cagney.

From there, James found work as a radio singer, then quickly managed to follow the trail that led to western film work. He signed up to shoot a series of films based on the radio series "Renfrew of the Royal Mounted," doing one film for Grand National and a second for Monogram. From there, he landed a

James Newill with Carol Hughes and Lightning in his 1937 film role as *Renfrew of the Royal Mounted*, Grand National.

spot in 1942 as one of the trio of cowboys in the PRC series *The Texas Rangers*. Along with Guy Wilkerson and Dave O'Brien, he made fourteen of these films, including *The Rangers Take Over* in 1942, *West of Texas* in 1943, and *Gunsmoke Mesa* in 1944. Newill and O'Brien also tried their hand at goat ranching while they were filming the series.

After a while, James had his singing minutes cut back by the producers. It wasn't long before he found himself replaced by another singing cowboy, the great star Tex Ritter. To his audiences, James suffered from much the same problem as George Houston. It was easier to picture him as an opera singer than a cowboy singer.

In 1945 he climbed down out of the saddle for a while and worked in

music performance. When he saddled up again, it was for television to make thirteen half-hour episodes of "Renfrew." Newill died in 1975. □

Newill is a Texas Ranger in *Return of the Rangers*, PRC, 1943.

SMITH BALLEW

Smith Ballew was born in 1911 in Palestine, Texas. Little is known about his childhood, and he is probably the most obscure of all the singing cowboys. The 1930s saw him rise to the peak of his popularity. Although he never attained prominence as a buckaroo balladeer, his career in films was impressive.

Ballew also has the distinction of being the only B-western star to work for Twentieth Century-Fox. In the early 1930s, he gained a following as a popular vocalist, orchestra leader, and recording artist for the

The talented Smith Ballew rose to fame as a top money-making western star in 1938, starring in a dozen oaters through 1951. Phillips Archives.

Columbia and Okeh labels.

A long controversy has brewed over whether Ballew's voice was dubbed for John Wayne's in the *Singin' Sandy* series. He appeared in Paramount's *Palm Springs* in 1936, and it was after this that producer Sol Lesser chose him as the cowboy for a western series produced by Twentieth Century-Fox.

Ballew cut a handsome figure on his horse Sheik, and he could carry his weight with cowboy ballads, but for some reason, the proof never came in at the box office. His featured singing-cowboy roles came in the films *Western Gold* (1937), *Panamint's Bad Man* (1938), *Roll Along Cowboy* (1938), *Rawhide* (1938), and *Hawaiian Buckaroo* (1938). □

$\mathcal{B}$OB BAKER

Of the cowboy heroes who rode the celluloid range, one who had done some real cowboying in his past was Bob Baker. He was born Stanley Leland Weed on November 8, 1914, in Forest City, Iowa. He was raised on cattle ranches in Arizona and Colorado, and it was while punching the Colorado cattle as a teenager that he gained the nickname "Tumble." After finishing school and working a number of odd jobs, he settled down into the world of rodeo, where he did quite well. Weed also had a passion for singing, and it wasn't long before he managed to become a performer at the "National Barn Dance."

In 1936 many young men were heading to California, guitar in hand, trying to join Hollywood's corral of singing cowboys. Weed is probably the only cowboy star who owes his first screen test to his mother. She heard of an opportunity at Universal Studios and sent his picture and a resume. In no time, Leland Weed received a letter from the studio and

In 1939 Universal's Bob Baker was among the top money-making western stars. Phillips Archives.

BOB BAKER IN

"HONOR OF THE WEST"

with Marjorie BELL · Carleton YOUNG · Jack KIRK

Directed by GEORGE WAGGNER · A NEW UNIVERSAL PICTURE · Produced by TREM CARR

Baker was two years into his Universal contract when he made *Honor of the West*, released in 1939. Phillips Archives.

made the trek to Tinsel Town. He won the job, even though other would-be singing cowboys tried out, including even Leonard Sly, who would later gain fame as Roy Rogers.

Contract in hand, Weed received coaching from another rodeo-rider-turned-Hollywood-cowboy, Max Terhune. In quintessential Hollywood fashion, Weed was given a horse, Apache, and saddled with a name better suited to a cowboy star: Bob Baker.

His first film was *Courage of the West*, made in 1937. Thanks to his tall, rugged looks and his ability to ride, rope and sing, his performance was given a favorable review. Unfortunately, he had a lot of competition and was never afforded the high-quality production, promotion, and especially coaching in acting that was given other warblers, namely, Gene Autry and Roy

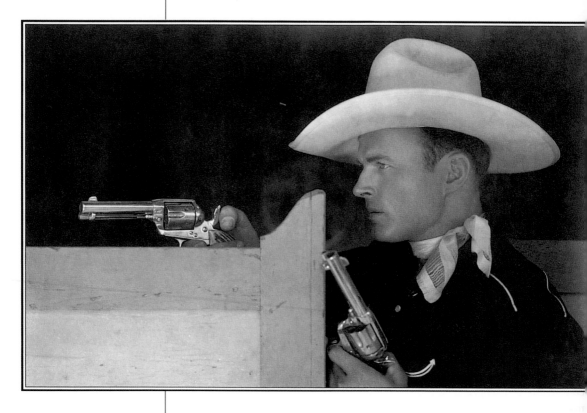

"The song's going to have to wait until these varmints are taken care of" appears to be Bob Baker's message in this publicity still. Phillips Archives.

Rogers. As a result, pleasant-voiced singing cowboy though he was, Baker's career never skyrocketed.

After starring in a dozen less-than-memorable serial films, Baker was reduced to riding alongside Johnny Mack Brown in Brown's westerns. He tried his luck at Monogram Studios in 1942 but received no bet-ter treatment there. After his final ride with Ken Maynard and Hoot Gibson in the 1943 Monogram pic-ture *Wild Horse Stampede*, Baker hung up his spurs for good. He died in 1975. Among his serial films were *The Last Stand*(1938), *Honor of the West* (1939), and *Bad Man From Red Butte* (1940). ☐

RAY WHITLEY

R ay Whitley never starred in any western film, but he still needs to be included in any account of the singing cowboy phenomenon for an important reason: he did as much as many stars to make the musical era a memorable one.

Several of the singing cowboys never starred in a musical western. They were but part of a group that made the films what they were. On the other hand, many of the starring saddle

Ray Whitley received sackloads of fan mail for his ability with a guitar and song, as evidenced in many B-westerns. Phillips Archives.

Cactus Mack. Far from least was Ray Whitley and his Bar 6 Cowboys.

Whitley was born in 1901 or 1902. He had put a group together in 1936 when the singing cowboy pictures were becoming the hot ticket. Ray and his Range Ramblers headed to Hollywood in hopes of a contract. He got a part in *Hopalong Cassidy Returns*, then landed with Tex Ritter in *Hittin' the Trail*. He had a contract that kept him busy for a long while. Still, the closest he ever came to being a true film "star" was in the musical shorts he began making in 1937. These mini-musicals lasted fifteen to twenty minutes each and eventually numbered nearly two dozen.

Ray also had a profitable recording contract with the ARC group, recording as Ray Whitley and as Whitley's Range Ramblers. He also cut a few sides with Odis Elder, such as "Have You Written Your Mother Lately?" and "The Wishing Well."

Everyone was impressed with this singing cowboy's ability, so RKO Pictures made him the singing sidekick of their number-one cowboy star, George O'Brien. Ray's group became known as the Bar 6 Cowboys, and the songs began pouring forth. There were five films made with third billing

aces couldn't carry a tune in a bucket and didn't even try. But even tone-deaf heroes needed musical interludes to compete in the sub-genre, and they were provided several highly talented singers and groups such as Bob Nolan and the Sons of the Pioneers, Foy Willing and the Riders of the Purple Sage, Spade Cooley and His Orchestra, Bob Wills and his Texas Playboys, Jimmy Wakely and his Saddle Pals,

for Whitley, just behind the star and the leading lady. This was a noteworthy achievement since, in most westerns, the supporting acts like Ray's were usually far down in the credits.

When cowboy Tim Holt took George O'Brien's place in 1940, Ray rode alongside him through a dozen films. By 1944 he was side-kicking for cowboy star Rod Cameron in the Universal corral.

Some of Ray's most memorable films over the years included *Rhythm Wranglers* (1937), *Gun Law* (1938), *Trouble in Sundown* (1939), *Wagon Train* (1940), *Cyclone on Horseback* (1941), *Thundering Hoofs* (1942), *Trigger Trail* (1944), and *Beyond the Pecos* (1945).

Ray was a fine actor and singer. He composed over two hundred country and western songs, including one that may well be the best-known song of its kind: Gene Autry's theme "Back in the Saddle Again." Ray was popular enough to be pictured in the western fan magazines of the 1940s, surrounded by heaps of fan mail. More than any other sagebrush musician, Ray Whitley possessed the talent necessary to ride the film's second-best horse and give the star moral and musical support that made a good film great. □

Ray Whitley doing what he did best, as he charms with song the attractive Virginia Vale in RKO's *Robbers of the Range,* 1941. Phillips Archives.

ROY ROGERS

Leonard Frank Sly, from Duck Run, Ohio: the name and place don't conjure the image of the white-hatted, hard-riding, straight-shooting, guitar-strumming man who came to be the most popular cowboy film star in history. But somehow the name Roy Rogers says it all.

Born in Cincinnati in 1911, Leonard Sly spent the first eight years of his life aboard a home-made riverboat before moving to the more rooted environment of Duck Run, up the Scioto River from Portsmouth. He spent a typical childhood, riding a bareback horse to school and raising a champion pig that took top honors at the county fair. It was a long trip from there to being the nation's number-one cowboy on the silver screen and under

The handsome young Roy Rogers decked out in Hollywood's finest western style.

the bright lights of the country's rodeo arenas.

His first step on that long road came when his family headed west in the midst of the Great Depression. Almost as soon as Leonard got the scent of ocean air and discovered that folks would pay their hard-earned nickels and dimes to hear him sing, he was sold on the life out west. He weathered some very hard times—picked peaches while living in the labor camps, drove trucks and worked on the highways, but he was determined, above all else, to make his mark in the entertainment industry.

Sly's perseverance finally paid off when he and some friends managed to find work singing original cowboy songs written by one of the group's members, the talented and prolific Bob Nolan. Stardom lay just ahead.

Now
52
pages!

Millions of Roy Rogers comics were sold between 1944 and 1962. Today they are highly collectible relics of a bygone era. Phillips Archives.

One of the numerous songbooks in Roger's career as a singing cowboy. Phillips Archives.

Lobby card for one of Roy's early movies. Phillips Archives.

First there were The Slye Brothers (Len and a cousin). Then Leonard and his buddies went through a number of name changes—from The Rocky Mountaineers, The O- Bar-O Cowboys, The Pioneer Trio, and others—before settling on The Sons of the Pioneers, the name given to them by an announcer on one of their early radio shows. Roy eventually left the group as his film career took off, but the group he helped found in 1933 went on to become the most successful cowboy harmony group of all time. It featured the vocal talents of Bob Nolan, Tim Spencer, Pat Brady, Lloyd Perryman, and others, as well as the extraordinary jazz-influenced guitar and fiddle work of Hugh and Karl Farr. The Sons of the Pioneers appeared in more than one hundred films, including many Roy Rogers titles, as well as made appearances on TV and at rodeos, state fairs, theaters, and nightclubs all over the U.S., Canada and overseas. Incorporating new members such as Ken Curtis, Dale Warren, Roy Lanham, and Rusty Richards as older members retired, The Sons of the Pioneers have seen tremendous success over several decades.

For himself, Leonard had even bigger goals, making screen tests and landing bit parts in films featuring Gene Autry and others. In 1938 Republic Studios renamed their singing cowboy phenomenon Roy Rogers, and placed him in his first leading role in *Under Western Stars*. By 1943, he had become the number-one western star, a position he held until there were no more polls to rank him, and he held the title of America's "King of the Cowboys" from then on. His horse Trigger became almost as big a star as he.

During this time, Roy had two marriages. His first one, to Lucile Acolese, was rocky and ended in divorce. His second marriage lasted ten years, until his wife Grace Arline died in 1946. Not long after that, Roy found true love in the form of a restless, ambitious spirit who was known by many names before achieving her ultimate stardom as Dale Evans. □

The Sons of the Pioneers became the most popular western singing group in history. Phillips Archives, Courtesy Katherine Smith Estate.

DALE EVANS

Roy Rogers's sweetheart was born October 30, 1912, in Uvalde, Texas, as Lucille Wood Smith (birth records) or on October 31 as Frances Octavia Smith (her parents' sworn affidavit). Frances, as she was known, spent the first seven years of her life on a farm in Italy, Texas, moving after that to Osceola, Arkansas, a town on the banks of the Mississippi.

At the age of fourteen, Frances eloped with a man a bit older than herself, calling her mother to announce that she would no longer be going by the name of Smith: it would now be Fox. The marriage was the beginning of a rocky existence that brought Frances three failed marriages and a son before she met her lasting love.

This publicity still captures the beauty that was Dale Evans, the most popular Hollywood cowgirl in history. Phillips Archives.

After suffering desertion and her first divorce, Frances was determined to raise her child on her own and gained work as a stenographer for an insurance company. Her boss overheard her singing and managed to get her on the radio. That first taste of professional performing got her hooked, and she began pursuing work in the entertainment industry. The early times were not easy, though, as she began and ended a second rocky marriage to August Johns and suffered from malnutrition and nervous problems.

Eventually, Frances located in Louisville, Kentucky, where she sang on WHAS Radio. There she was given her show names Marion Lee, then Dale Evans. Making thirty dollars a week, Dale met and, after relocating to Dallas, married her third

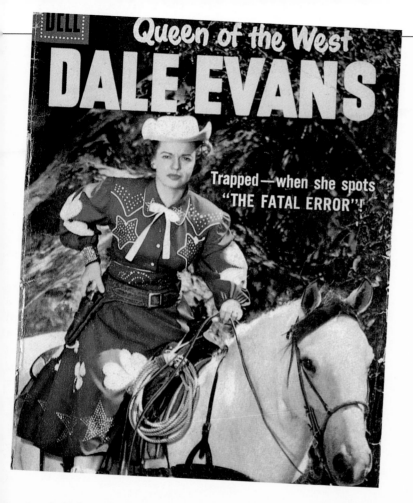

Queen of the West
DALE EVANS

Trapped—when she spots "THE FATAL ERROR"!

husband, Robert Butts, a music arranger who followed her wherever she found work as her career really started to take off over the next few years.

Dale performed over Dallas radio and made personal appearances in Texas, then relocated to Chicago to find work in nightclubs, ritzy hotels, and on the CBS Radio airwaves, holding down her own show called "That Gal From Texas." Climbing the ladder of success, she was soon given the chance to do a screen test in Hollywood. The Tinsel Town wheels were not happy to learn she was the mother of a teenaged son, but Dale relocated to California after agreeing to pass the boy off as her younger brother.

Although her first tryouts were disappointing, she finally signed on the dotted line at Twentieth Century Fox. Nothing spectacular happened at first, especially after her agent entered the armed forces. But she wound up with the same agent who was handling the up-and-coming sensation Roy Rogers. Roy got most of the agent's attention, though, and the agent in turn got Dale's fury. Dale finally fired her agent and hired another who, ironically, brought her close to Roy Rogers once again by securing a contract for her at Republic, the film studio that was handling Roy. She made *Swing Your Partner* and nine more films in rapid succession, including *Here Comes Elmer* and *Hoosier Holiday.* Her first western was with John Wayne, *War of the Wild-cats.* Even more important for her future as a star, she finally met Roy in person for the first time during a show at Edwards Air Force Base. □

THE COWBOY KING & QUEEN

D ale Evans once wrote and recorded the song, "I'll Never Fall in Love With a Cowboy." She did fall in love with one, though—the most famous one in the world—and for both of them it was the biggest turning point in their lives.

The nearly mythic partnership of Roy and Dale took root when Republic head Herbert Yates decided to cast the two together in the film *The Cowboy and the Senorita*. The pairing seemed natural, and Dale became part of Roy's touring road shows and soon joined him on network radio. She resisted pressure to make her into a female saddle ace, however, complaining that "a heroine in a western is always second string. The cowboy and his horse always come

Roy and Dale in publicity still for *Lights of Old Santa Fe,* 1944. This was Dale's first year of starring with Roy in films, three years before they were wed. Phillips Archives.

first." She continued to find casting in other types of films. But in spite of her protests, everything was "Roy and Dale," and fans begged Republic to keep her saddled up with Roy.

In October 1946, Roy's second wife gave birth to a baby boy and a few days later left him a widower. In November, Dale's third marriage ended in divorce. Roy and Dale's work kept them together almost constantly, and their relationship naturally blossomed into a full-fledged romance. Although Dale was still not happy with her work at Republic, word leaked out about the romance, and the two were married December 31, 1947 on the ranch where they had filmed the picture *Home in Oklahoma.*

Roy and Dale's trials and joys centered around their children. There

Roy Rogers and Dale Evans pictured on the cover of one of the many pieces of sheet music issued throughout their careers. Phillips Archives. Copyright Paramount-Roy Rogers Music Co., Inc.

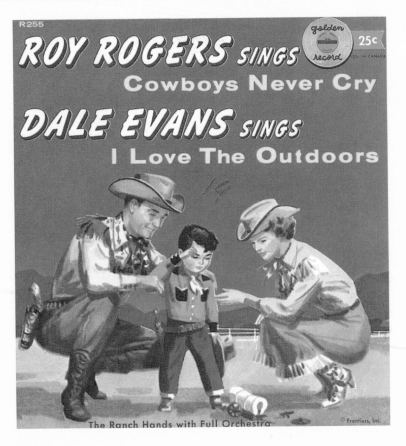

R255

ROY ROGERS SINGS
Cowboys Never Cry
DALE EVANS SINGS
I Love The Outdoors

golden record 25¢

25c IN CANADA

The Ranch Hands with Full Orchestra

© Frontiers, Inc.

Roy and Dale recorded for young and old alike. Their Little Golden Records for children represented millions in sales. Phillips Archives. (Little Golden Records trademark owned by Western Publishing Co., Inc.).

would be many: three from Roy's previous marriage to Arline and Dale's grown son at college, for a start. The pair became parents to their own little girl, who lived only two years, then they adopted an

Indian girl and a handicapped boy who met with an accidental death while stationed in Germany in the army. While on tour of the British Isles in 1954, they became foster parents to a girl from Scotland. Finally, they adopted a little Korean/Puerto Rican girl, who died in a bus accident in 1964. Through all the joys and tragedies, they were held together by their strong commitment to each other, to their faith in God, to their family and to their work.

Down through the years, the couple never lost sight of their fans. Many people now remember Roy and Dale best for their television show, which saw more than a hundred episodes introduced by Dale's hit composition "Happy Trails." There were commercial tie-ins for both Roy and Dale that outdid everything Hollywood had to offer short of Walt Disney himself—products like comic books, lunch boxes, clothing, and play sets that today command ever-increasing prices from collectors of western memorabilia. The awards and citations Roy and Dale received over the years were enough to fill a museum, which they did in the 1960s.

In addition to more than eighty sagebrush films and countless appearances, Roy and Dale held

down major recording careers of hundreds of songs. Dale became the only female star to be included in *Motion Picture Magazine*'s list of the top money-making western stars. She has authored more than twenty books teaching others to face life's difficult struggles and lessons. Over forty-six years of riding side by side in the public eye, Roy and Dale have truly earned the title of America's favorite western couple. □

Dale Evans, Pat Brady, and Roy Rogers in a still for *Bells of Coronado*, 1950. Phillips Archives.

GEORGE HOUSTON

George Houston was born in 1898 in Hampton, New Jersey, the son of a minister. He attended Rutgers and Julliard universities and served in the United States Army during World War I. On returning to civilian life, he opened a voice school in New York City and joined the American Opera Company, performing on Broadway.

By 1934 Hollywood beckoned and George responded, landing a part in *The Melody Lingers On.* He then starred as Wild Bill Hickok in Grand National's *Frontier Scout* in 1938. In 1940 he appeared in *The Howards of Virginia* for Columbia Pictures. The next year, with his

Houston entertains his fellow buckaroos in this still from his *Lone Rider in Ghost Town* movie, PRC, 1941.

horse Lightnin' and Al St. John for a sidekick, he became PRC's singing cowboy in *The Lone Rider* series, which lasted for eleven pictures.

Houston possessed a dynamic singing voice but was never quite comfortable with the singing-cowboy roles. Nor was he able to make the adjustment enough to suit fans of the horse operas, for it was said that he sounded like a classical singer, decked out in cowboy hat

and boots. Wrangler Bob Livingston eventually took George's place in *The Lone Rider* series.

Houston's films included *The Lone Rider Rides On* and *The Lone Rider in Frontier Fury* in 1941, then *The Lone Rider in Cheyenne* and *Outlaws of Boulder Pass* in 1942. In the end, though, it may be that he cared more for the opera stage than a seat in the saddle. When George died of a heart attack at age forty-five or forty-six, he was working with The New York Theatre Guild, organizing an opera division. □

George Houston looks formidable enough to handle both of these bad guys. Still from *Frontier Scout*, a 1938 Fine Arts/Grand National adventure film.

TEX FLETCHER

ex Fletcher became one of the few left-handed guitar pickers ever to appear in a western film. He had a recording career as well. Tex Fletcher's Lonely Cowboys recorded numerous issues for the Decca label, some with Tex's partner Joe Rogers. He got his start in show business as a performer with Buffalo Bill's Wild West show, then got work as a radio singer in Yankton, South Dakota, billed as "The Lonely Cowboy." He went back home to New York, where he began singing over WOR Radio, a spot he held for six years. Most of his songs were tearjerkers, telling of unrequited love.

Tex was born Jerry Bisceglia in Harrison, New York, 1909. He rode onto the Hollywood range in several musical shorts for E. W. Hammonds, the head of Grand National Pictures. Then in 1939, he filmed *Six Gun Rhythm*, his first and only shoot-'em-up for Grand National, which was having financial difficulties at the time. The studio folded just as the movie was being released, a black-and-white entry with Ralph Peters as the singing cowboy's sidekick.

Despite the upset, Tex proved his skin tough as leather when confronted with the circumstances. He took off to New England, working as his own promoter for the film. He managed to win exposure for it and many personal appearances for himself as well. Undoubtedly, he could have picked up his saddle and cut a deal at another studio, but World War II broke out, and he had to swap his six-gun for an M-1 rifle to serve in the United States Army.

Upon discharge, Tex returned to his New York radio show and

TEX
FLETCHER

hosted some obscure local television shows during the 1950s and 1960s. Tex Fletcher, who goes in the record book as the only one-film singing cowboy, died in 1986. ☐

Tex Fletcher had the shortest film career of any of the singing cowboys, making only one film. Phillips Archives, courtesy Katherine Smith Estate.

PATSY MONTANA

When Patsy Montana's recording of "I Wanna Be a Cowboy's Sweetheart" hit the airwaves in 1936, it was the first million seller ever recorded by a woman country singer, and it paved the way for countless other women in country music and carved out a name for Patsy Montana. A dynamic singer with a wide-brimmed cowgirl hat and plentiful fringes, Patsy made over two hundred recordings, enjoyed dozens of big hits, performed as a regular on the "National Barn Dance" for twenty-five years, and took the art—cowboy yodeling and song—to new heights. She also became one of the very few singing cowgirls to make her mark in the Hollywood westerns of the 1940s.

Patsy Montana yodeled her way to fame, paving the way for many future singing cowgirls. She appeared in Gene Autry's *Colorado Sunset*. Phillips Archives, courtesy Patsy Montana .

Patsy Montana started life as Ruby Blevins in Hot Springs, Arkansas, on October 30, 1914. She grew up listening to the same legendary singers who influenced most of the stars of her profession: Jimmie Rogers, the Mississippi Blue Yodeler, and Gene Autry. She had no female role models—there were almost no women in country music at the time.

She spent her high school and college years sharpening her skills, working on the guitar and fiddle, and adding song after song to her repertoire. With two other girls she formed a trio, The Montana Cowgirls, and took the name Patsy at the suggestion of Stuart Hamblin, a popular singer at the time. It wasn't long before she had signed a recording contract and in 1933 began seeing success with releases

WELLS FARGO THEATER

such as "When the Flowers of Montana are Blooming" and "I Love My Daddy, Too." On a trip to the Chicago World's Fair, Patsy's mother encouraged her to say hello to some of her favorite singers on WLS Radio's "National Barn Dance." Soon, she was fronting WLS's popular string band, The

Today Patsy is recognized as an institution in country and western music. Phillips Archives, courtesy Patsy Montana.

She made a huge contribution toward popularizing the image of the American cowgirl. Phillips Archives, courtesy Patsy Montana and Bruce Fischer.

music festivals and special gatherings. The legendary yodeler and singer of such hits as "I'm an Old Cowhand," "Singing in the Saddle," "Cowboy Rhythm," and "Ridin' the Sunset Trail" still packs 'em in. Indisputably the first cowgirl of song, Patsy Montana has found her place in the history books as one of western music's all-time greats. □

Patsy still draws crowds today, singing the songs that made her and her buckaroo friends famous. Phillips Archives, courtesy Patsy Montana and Bruce Fischer. Copyright Flying Fish Records, Inc.

In 1970, along with Tex Ritter, Patsy received the Pioneer Award from the Academy of Music.

Prairie Ramblers.

Gene Autry was also a part of the WLS show for a spell. After establishing himself in Hollywood, Gene helped Patsy break another gender barrier, asking her to appear in a couple of his films, including *Colorado Sunset* (1939). Patsy went on to make several musical shorts of that type.

Throughout the 1940s and 50s, the singer with the voice as big as Montana made many television appearances and toured heavily, incorporating her two little girls into the act. She even had her own radio program, "Wake Up and Smile," on ABC. She slowed down somewhat during the 1960s, but still maintained a performing schedule and won over college-aged fans. Along with Tex Ritter, she became a recipient of the Academy of Country Music's Pioneer Award in 1970.

Today Patsy still records and makes appearances at western

JOHN "DUSTY" KING

John "Dusty" King was born Miller McLeod Everson on July 11, 1909, in Cincinnati, Ohio. As a young man, he attended the University of Cincinnati. After a start in the entertainment world on the radio—first as an announcer, then as a singer—he landed a position as vocalist for Ben Bernie's Orchestra. Several musical shorts provided his first exposure on celluloid.

His first real acting was in the 1934 serial "The Adventures of Frank Merriwell" and the 1936 serial "Ace Drummond." King also appeared in several musical comedies, including "Three Smart Girls Grow Up." He went on to become the singing cowboy member of The Range Busters for Monogram

John "Dusty" King posing for a publicity still for one of his western films.

The Range Busters
RAY (CRASH) CORRIGAN
JOHN (DUSTY) KING
MAX (ALIBI) TERHUNE

IN FUGITIVE VALLEY

King and saddle pard Ray "Crash" Corrigan strike a jovial pose in the lobby card for Monogram's 1941 *Fugitive Valley*. Phillips Archives.

Pictures in 1940, sharing the billing with saddle pals Ray "Crash" Corrigan and Max Terhune, then with David Sharpe, who took Corrigan's place. During a three-year period, King appeared in twenty of these trio westerns (which numbered twenty-four), handling the warbling chores. After this series ended, he appeared in a few more films until 1946, when he retired from the screen.

Some of King's singing cowboy films were: *Trailing Double Trouble* in 1940, *Fugitive Valley* in 1941, *Thunder River Feud* in 1942, and *Two-Fisted* in 1943. □

BOB WILLS

James Robert Wills was born to play a fiddle if anyone ever was. His grandfather played, his father played, even his aunts and uncles played the fiddle. His dad was a championship fiddler who competed against the best. Sometimes when his dad would hit the jug too heavily, ten-year-old Bob would take his place at the house dances. Often the two would play side by side. They would travel for miles around and folks would

The Tiffany transcriptions represent some of the most exciting sounds ever recorded by Wills. Kaleidoscope issued ten volumes on album, which are now seeing re-release by Rhino Records. On this cover, Bob is astride his second horse, Black Diamond. Phillips Archives. Courtesy/copyright Kaleidoscope Records.

KALEIDOSCOPE F-32

Bob Wills AND HIS TEXAS PLAYBOYS

THE TIFFANY TRANSCRIPTIONS VOL. 8

Trouble In Mind
Blues For Dixie
There's Gonna Be A Party
Sioux City Sue
Sitting On Top Of The World
Stash
My Confusion

Little Liza Jane
Miss Molly
Ten Years
Twinkle Twinkle Little Star
Big Beaver
Cindy
Sun Bonnet Sue

More of the Best

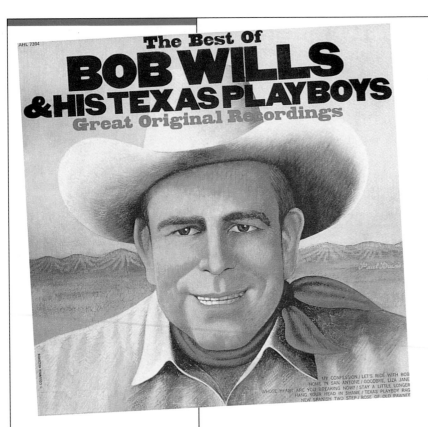

AHL 7304

The Best Of
BOB WILLS
& HIS TEXAS PLAYBOYS
Great Original Recordings

MY CONFESSION / LET'S RIDE WITH BOB
HOME IN SAN ANTONE / GOODBYE, LIZA JANE
WHOSE HEART ARE YOU BREAKING NOW? / STAY A LITTLE LONGER
HANG YOUR HEAD IN SHAME / TEXAS PLAYBOY RAG
NEW SPANISH TWO STEP / ROSE OF OLD PAWNEE

The majority of Bob Wills's 500 plus recordings have been issued on albums such as this one from Columbia Records. Courtesy/copyright CBS Records. Phillips Archives.

Bob also borrowed from the songs he heard working in his family's cotton fields, from the blues he heard sung in town streets and from popular recording artists such as blues singer Bessie Smith.

Bob worked as a barber for a while but was determined to make his living as a musician. He met guitarist Herman Arnspiger, and the two landed a job playing over WBAP Radio in Ft. Worth, Texas. Radio paid nothing, but it gave Bob a chance to pitch his act, become well known, and increase his bookings. Bob and Herman soon hooked up with a flour company in Texas, performing as The Light Crust Doughboys. Bob put up with a domineering owner for about a year but finally left the Doughboys and took a number of the other musicians with him. The band eventually found a permanent home on KVOO Radio in Tulsa, Oklahoma, as the Texas Playboys.

The band eventually grew so large that Bob and his brother Johnnie Lee split the group to cover more than one place at a time. Johnnie Lee took charge of the Tulsa activities, while Bob and another bus load of boys took off for California. Their immense popularity soon blanketed the entire Southwest.

push the furniture aside and dance right up until the break of dawn.

The Wills family played "Texas fiddle," a style that differed from the Anglo-Scots-Irish traditions, one that wound and slurred through hundreds of blues, jazz, Dixieland, old-time fiddle tunes, old cowboy ballads, and even popular songs.

In the early 1940s Bob's group was filling dance halls and making many hit records. In 1940 he signed with Monogram Pictures and was featured in *Take Me Back to Oklahoma*, a film made with fellow-Texan Tex Ritter. The contract allowed for him and five musicians, including the legendary Eldon Shamblin on guitar and Leon McAuliffe on steel guitar.

Bob got to use his entire big band in Glenn Ford's *Go West Young Lady*, a Columbia film. Cindy Walker, the now-renowned Texas songwriter, began writing songs for Bob's band, further strengthening their appeal with classic-style

Wills and some of his Texas Playboys appeared in several western films, providing the musical interludes. To Bob's right is renowned fiddler Jesse Ashlock. Phillips Archives.

cowboy ballads such as "Dusty Skies." She wrote the songs for eight Columbia films featuring Wills and the boys that cemented the western image of the Texas fiddler and band leader.

In films and appearances Bob was always seen in the fine western tradition: white Stetson and boots. A big cigar became his trademark. Often he was astride his beloved horse Punkin. Western style was a look and manner all the Texas Playboys adopted, and since several even mastered the art of roping, it was only natural that a group with such talent would wind up on the silver screen.

At its largest, the Texas Playboys comprised an unheard-of twenty-two pieces, including fiddles, horns, reeds, drums, and various guitars: steel, doghouse bass, rhythm, and lead. Bob set records for crowds everywhere he played. He even outdrew major big-city swing bands like those of Tommy Dorsey and Benny Goodman. His brothers were keeping them dancing back in Oklahoma and even up in northern California, where brother Billy Jack commanded a group. He was even buying ballrooms to further promote the Wills industry.

The advent of television and a bad business venture were the beginning of the end for Bob's big-band days. His ruin finally came when he bought a large dance hall in Dallas, the Bob Wills Ranch House. Poor management and dishonest employees put him under a tremendous financial strain, just as television was pulling fans away from the dance halls and movie theaters. Bob headed back to Tulsa in the early fifties and joined his group with those of his brothers, Johnnie Lee and Luke, attempting to draw crowds through sheer quantity and quality of talent.

Bob was never satisfied in one spot and eventually took off for Las Vegas, where the band worked casinos and continued their touring. Constant traveling, several stormy marriages, and a drinking problem was taking a toll on his health. A heart attack in 1962 and another two years later forced him to give up the band for good, but there was no way to quiet Bob's fiddle. He continued to front other bands, taking advantage of his own tremendous following and making some big door takes for fellow band leaders such as Hoyle Nix.

During 1968 and '69 Bob was elected into the Country Music Hall of Fame, inducted into the National Cowboy Hall of Fame and honored by the Texas legislature. The day after he received this last honor, Bob suffered a stroke that left him partially paralyzed and speech-impaired.

Bob Wills's recording career took in over 550 songs and instrumentals, many becoming standards in country and western music: "San Antonio Rose," "Steel Guitar Rag," "Take Me Back to Tulsa," "Faded Love," "Roly Poly." He had become a living legend.

In December 1973 he realized a dream when numerous former Texas Playboys gathered for a jam session in Bob's living room and the next day began to record a United Artists album entitled *For the Last Time*. Bob managed to get his trademark "Ahh-haa" in all the right places, including a fond tribute Cindy Walker wrote for the occasion, "What Makes Bob Holler?" That night he had a second stroke and another two days later. On the second day of recording, the session was finished without him and there wasn't a dry eye in the studio.

Bob remained in a coma, and when he died eighteen months later in a Ft. Worth nursing home, his wife fulfilled his final wish, "Take Me Back to Tulsa." □

BILL BOYD

With 229 recordings for Victor, of which 227 were released, Bill Boyd had one of the most successful musical careers of all the singing cowboy stars. His 1935 recording of Wagner's "Under the Double Eagle" became a country-music classic and a standard for countless other performers. "Beaumont Rag," "Boyd's Tin Roof Blues," "New Fort Worth Rag," "Lone Star Rag," "Beale Street Blues," "Right or Wrong," "Wah Hoo"—Bill Boyd and his Cowboy Ramblers produced an impressive string of great hits.

Born on September 29, 1910, in Fannin County, Texas, William Lemuel Boyd grew up among a family of fifteen, working a 320-acre cattle ranch and cotton farm. Bill and his brothers spent a number of years roping and riding as working cowboys, helping keep the family business in order.

The family enjoyed listening to a

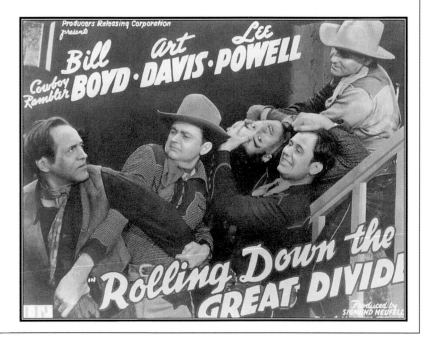

BILL BOYD
AND HIS COWBOY RAMBLERS'
FOLIO OF WESTERN SONGS
No. 1

Containing 20 ORIGINAL SONGS COMPLETE WITH WORDS AND MUSIC, GUITAR UKULELE AND BANJO CHORDS

Bill Boyd and his famous horse, Texas?

50¢
MADE IN U.S.A.

AMERICAN MUSIC, INC.
STUDIO BUILDING   PORTLAND, ORE.

battery-powered radio and playing popular 78-rpm recordings on their Victrola-style phonograph. Bill sent off for a mail-order guitar, and soon he and his brother Jim became proficient enough to land a job on a local radio show over KFPM in Greenville. Radio certainly didn't pay much in 1926, but it taught the boys that there was more pleasure to be found singing and playing than working the fields.

Bill's first break came after the family moved to Dallas in 1929. He and two of his buddies—harmonica player O. P. Alexander and mandolinist Red Stevens—auditioned for radio station WFAA. With Bill singing and playing guitar, they won a slot on the station's morning show, calling their band Alexander's Daybreakers. Meanwhile, at the local high school, brother Jim met up with Art Davis, a clarinet player who soon expanded his talents to the fiddle and mandolin, and the two began performing for school programs.

By 1932 Bill's band had combined with Jim's, and the Cowboy Ramblers were born. In the dark days of the Great Depression, the boys achieved enormous popularity playing over Dallas radio station WRR, and in 1934 signed a recording contract with the Victor Company that would keep them busy for the next seventeen years. At the Texas Hotel in San Antonio on August 7, the band recorded their first fiddle tunes and songs, including "The Strawberry Roan."

By the early 1940s, many young men like Bill were migrating to Hollywood, looking for exposure in film. Bill had made enough hit records to cause important people to take notice. His manager, Jack Adams, convinced PRC to take a chance on Bill as their new singing cowboy star. Bill landed starring roles in the films *Texas Manhunt, Raiders of the West, Rolling Down the Great Divide, Tumbleweed Trail, Prairie Pals,* and *Along the Sundown Trail.* He was billed as Bill "Cowboy Rambler" Boyd, and sometimes called Bill "Radio" Boyd to distinguish him from the other popular Bill Boyd, better known as Hopalong Cassidy, and still another Hollywood actor by the same name.

Bill Boyd's six films were all

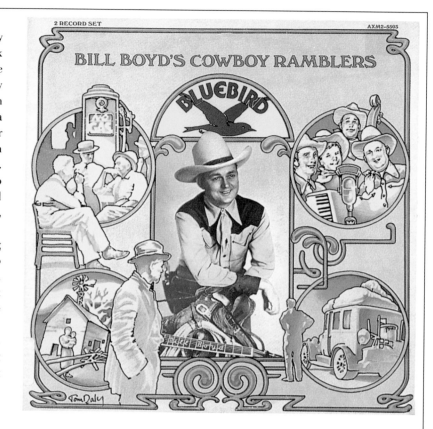

2 RECORD SET

AXM2-5503

BILL BOYD'S COWBOY RAMBLERS

BLUEBIRD

Tom Daly

made during 1942, but he performed music until he was forced to stop after suffering a stroke in 1973. He died December 7, 1977. In spite of his memorable film work, Bill will always be remembered best as the "King of the Instrumentals." □

"Radio" and "Cowboy Rambler" were nicknames necessary to keep Bill Boyd from being confused with the two other Bill Boyds in Hollywood, including "Hopalong Cassidy." These shots are from his early singing cowboy years. His horse was Texas. Phillips Archives, courtesy Katherine Smith Estate.

EDDIE DEAN

H e was one of the top ten western stars in the 1940s—a tough corral to get into at the time. In the opinion of many, Eddie was by far the best singer of all the musical cowboys.

For one with so prestigious a career, little has been written of his childhood and early professional life. He was born in Posey, Texas, July 9, 1907, and began his career in the late 1920s, touring the Midwest as part of a quartet. By the early thirties, he was singing on WIBW Radio in Topeka with his

Dean had several horses during his film-making career, among them Copper, Flash, and White Cloud. Phillips Archives.

brother Jimmy (not to be confused with the Jimmy Dean of "Big Bad John" and breakfast-sausage fame).

Also in the thirties, Eddie landed acting parts in CBS radio "soap operas" produced in Chicago. While there, he also worked the popular "National Barn Dance" show broadcast over WLS throughout the Midwest and parts of the South and East.

At the suggestion of his radio-show writer, Eddie almost headed to New York for work in musical comedies. But his main ambition was to get into radio as a singer, so in 1937 he headed for sunny California instead, where the biggest shows were being done. He came close to getting a spot on the "Jack Benny Show" but was beat out by Dennis Day. The producers of the show wanted a tenor.

Looking for work anywhere he could find it, Eddie found it singing in nightclubs. He also got a job as a vocalist on Judy Canova's radio show, all the while making the rounds of studios looking for work in cowboy pictures. As a youngster, his idol had been cowboy star Hoot Gibson, and he felt working in westerns was something that could make him happy.

In the late summer of 1938, Eddie

impressed a casting director at Republic Pictures with his script reading and also persuaded the director that he could ride anything they had. So they put him in the waiting wings. When the big break finally came, Eddie appeared in *Western Jamboree*. According to Dean, he must have gone on to appear in a hundred films for Republic, all in supporting roles. Existing filmographies list at least

Eddie Dean is about to tangle with Al "Lash" LaRue in this still from his 1945 *Song of Old Wyoming*. Phillips Archives.

Dean made fifty-two films and has been called the "number one singing cowboy." This scene is from the PRC film *West to Glory*. Phillips Archives.

1944 film *The White Stallion*, but it was a deal he made in 1945 to appear in color films that really turned the tide for him. He met a fellow who was trying to sell his Cinecolor process to the industry, trying to compete with the Technicolor monopoly. He offered Eddie a year's contract with PRC (Producer's Releasing Corporation) in return for help marketing the product.

In *Song of Old Wyoming*, Eddie became a singing cowboy star in his own right, with the distinction of being the first to film in color. PRC garnered a million bucks and made Dean an industry force to reckon with in his first series oater. Although there were numerous singing cowboys on the back lots, they were mostly being seen in black and white.

Eddie made about twenty feature westerns on his horse Flash, with pretty leading ladies like Sarah Padden, Shirley Patterson, Peggy Wynn, and most often, Jennifer Holt. Beyond his great singing, he distinguished himself in films by doing some of his own stunt work: the fight scenes and falls from his horse.

Eddie secured a recording contract in the 1940s, and that began a back-to-back career with acting. He

thirty of them. Eddie was even seen in the 1939 serial *The Lone Ranger Rides Again*, starring Bob Livingston, which earned him a solid paycheck for a good thirteen weeks. Dean appeared in the films of Gene Autry, Roy Rogers, Bob Steele, Don "Red" Barry, and Lee Powell. There were even nine Hopalong Cassidy outings, and he contributed greatly to the worthiness of some of the films by adding a song or two of his own.

Eddie shared top billing with Ken Maynard and Max Terhune in the

was an accomplished songwriter, composing about a hundred songs. His biggest-selling song was "One Has My Name, The Other Has My Heart," which was also recorded by the likes of Jimmy Wakely, who had a sizable hit with it. Eddie's lifelong wife, Lorene, ("Dearest") had a hand in this one, as she did with numerous others. Another monster hit was "I Dreamed of a Hillbilly Heaven," which was recorded by Tex Ritter and many others. Today

Eddie is probably best remembered for his singing of "Wagon Wheels." Many of the title songs for his films were written by him and Hal Blair, among them "Stars Over Texas" and "West to Glory."

In his search for hit records, Eddie's biggest drawback was issuing them on independent labels, such as his own Sage and Sand label. Lacking good distribution, his songs usually had more success when recorded by other artists.

Eddie Dean was still working nightclubs, fairs, and special events into the late 1970s. In the eighties, when western film festivals became popular, he could often be found in attendance—the tall, lanky cowboy with the friendly, weathered face, his wife "Dearest" on his arm, playing host to a legion of fans.

Even in his golden years, rounding out a career of over five decades, Eddie could still play the guitar and sing to knock 'em dead. ☐

Eddie Dean appears to have the situation under control in this still from his 1948 Eagle-Lion film *Check Your Guns*. Phillips Archives.

JIMMY WAKELY

In 1927, when Jimmy Wakely was thirteen, his family moved from the hills of Oklahoma to the west side of the state, where they began farming and picking cotton. Soon after, the horrible black storms of the dust bowl days wiped out farm after farm. Thousands of Okies migrated west to escape the storms and poverty. Others, like the Wakely family, headed back to the hills, hauling their pigs, chickens, and personal belongings on a Model T Ford.

One day, far removed from the hard times, Jimmy recalled his childhood in a song:

My daddy was a workin' man,
part time at the mill;
My uncle had a better job;
he ran a whiskey still.

Wakely and his horse, Sunset, strike a typical cowboy publicity pose. Phillips Archives.

The whistle of that lonesome train made chills run up my spine—
But how can a young man get away,
when he hasn't got a dime?

Things went from bad to worse. Money got scarce, and the family's hogs died of cholera. Jimmy managed to work for five bucks several days a month, but when the family well went dry in 1933 and he caught malaria from the invading mosquitoes, Jimmy swore he'd find a way to escape what he had come to consider a rural ghetto.

One of his escapes was through his deep attachment to music. He would sit out on the porch and imitate the "blue yodels" of Jimmie Rodgers, the singing brakeman who often sang of trains and the adven-

tures to which they could carry you.

After the family moved once again, to Rosedale, Jimmy found some neighbor boys to play music with and eventually married the sister of one. He also found another

big musical influence in the popular vocalist Milton Brown, leader of the Musical Brownies. Brown helped create and popularize a type of music that incorporated old-time fiddle tunes, hot city jazz, and even

Wakely comes to the defense of this woman's honor in *Song of the Drifter*, 1948. Phillips Archives.

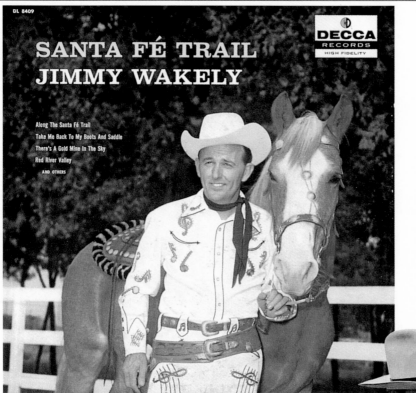

cowboy songs into what became known as western swing.

With some piano experience, Jimmy got a job on the weekends playing with Merle Salathiel and his Barnyard Boys for $6.00. He supplemented that with a singing job for $2.50 a week at KTOK in Oklahoma City, where he added cowboy songs to his professional repertoire.

In the summer of 1937, Jimmy landed work with Little Doc Roberts' Medicine Show, playing the towns around Oklahoma City while his wife hawked tonic to the audiences. His biggest break came when he was offered a job singing with a trio known

Jimmy Wakely was one of the few who dared to go all out in Hollywood glitz, as is evident in this photo used for his Decca Records album *Santa Fe Trail*. **Phillips Archives. Courtesy/copyright MCA Records.**

Wakely in an action publicity still for one of his western films. **Phillips Archives.**

as the Bell Boys over WKY Radio. Jimmy pulled his friend Johnny Bond into the act—a talented singer and guitarist. Rounded out by Scotty Harrell, the group could be heard on the radio five days a week.

Fronting what had now become the Jimmy Wakely Trio, Jimmy got a chance to lead the band for his favorite cowboy singer, Gene Autry. He even had the job of setting up Gene's music. The band changed its name once more to Jimmy Wakely and the Melody Ranch Boys and went out with Gene to tour the rodeo circuit.

It wasn't long before Jimmy had wrangled motion-picture work with his trio, landing supporting roles in the films of Roy Rogers, Gene Autry, Hopalong Cassidy, Johnny Mack Brown and Tex Ritter, Charles Starrett, and The Range Busters. After more than a dozen supporting roles, he finally got a starring role in the 1944 Monogram film *Song of the Range*. Wakely managed to outgun the studio's Cisco Kid titles, but a production manager who had stock in the company's Johnny Mack Brown features caught Jimmy up in a deal intended to make Brown come out on top. Though he was beating Brown at the box office, Jimmy was forced to cut back on his music, his costuming, and even had to give up his fancy Bohlin-type silver saddle.

Nevertheless, Jimmy went on to make twenty-eight black-and-white pictures for Monogram, featuring sidekicks such as Lee "Lasses" White and Dub "Cannonball" Taylor, and pretty leading ladies like Virginia Belmont and Mildred Coles.

Jimmy's great voice allowed him to jump over into the recording industry after 1949, when competition from television began creating problems for B-western cowboys. In that year, he recorded a duet with Margaret Whiting for Capitol Records—"Slippin' Around." The song hit number one on the charts, and Jimmy had a new career on more solid ground. His cover of Eddie Dean's "One Has My Name, The Other Has My Heart" shot to the number-one position in six weeks, and he placed over twenty songs on the charts during the next couple of years. Jimmy became an accomplished songwriter and got his own radio show on CBS that ran from 1952 to 1958, outlasting Gene Autry's network show by two years.

Jimmy wrote many of the songs that were used in his films, but he recorded very few of them himself. He wrote "The Weary Stranger" that he sang in the 1954 film *Arrow in the Dust*. He wrote "Silver Star" and sang it off-camera in the film of that title. He also wrote a few songs for Jock Mahoney films which include "Cowboy" and "Lonely is the Hunter."

Jimmy occasionally returned to the film screen through 1959 to give forth with a song. In the 1960s and '70s, he worked on television and in nightclubs. By the late 1970s, Jimmy was celebrating his tenth year with Armed Forces Radio with a daily show over Radio Iran. In partnership with Autry, he was also producing half-hour television shows for broadcast in Iran.

Since Wakely's death in 1982, his memory has been kept alive by a very loyal fan, H. D. Martin, who bought out the estate in 1984—from the clothing and gun belt to the 1976 Cadillac Fleetwood Brougham that was Jimmy's final touring car—and opened a Wakely museum. Martin also formed the Jimmy Wakely Fan Club and toured the western film festivals to honor the memory of a man who rose from the impoverished Oklahoma hills to become one of the country's favorite singing cowboys. □

$\mathcal{K}$EN CURTIS

Curtis Gates was born in July 1916 in southeastern Colorado and was raised in Lamar. Appropriately, his father was a sheriff. Later, Curtis himself would best be remembered as a lawman, co-starring in the classic television series "Gunsmoke." But that was his second or third trail to fame. Though many fans don't realize it, Curtis was once one of the notable singing cowboys of the B-westerns.

While his dad was enforcing the law in Bent County, Colorado, Curtis literally grew up in jail, the building where his family made their home. Curtis helped his dad by working as a jail keeper, and his mother's cooking fed both his family and the prisoners. Later, he got involved with ranching and farming—appropriate enough for a future cowboy star. He also took

In the nine musical westerns Ken Curtis made for Columbia, he seemed to spend more time singing than chasing the bad guys. Phillips Archives.

up, of all things, the saxophone. It was an unusual beginning, but music was to shape the life and career of this Colorado lad.

Although Curtis studied medicine for a time at Colorado College, his love for music was a stronger force, and he found his way to Hollywood, where he obtained work as staff singer on NBC Radio. His timing could not have been better; soon, the great band leader Tommy Dorsey hired him to replace Frank Sinatra, who had decided to strike out on his own. It was a great compliment to Curtis's way with a song and an equal testament to his versatility that he also ended up a member of a western group on its way to becoming the most popular in history, the Sons of the Pioneers.

Curtis served in World War II and upon his discharge quickly resumed his music career. Numerous radio

Ken Curtis in a publicity
still with Amanda Blake
from "Gunsmoke."
Phillips Archives.
Copyright CBS, Inc.

**Ken Curtis as Festus Haggen with Milburn Stone from "Gunsmoke."
Phillips Archives. Copyright CBS, Inc.**

as Gene Autry and Roy Rogers, thrilling audiences across the land.

Ken Curtis made feature westerns with titles like *Swing in the Saddle*, *Rhythm Roundup*, *That Texas Jamboree*, and *Singing on the Trail*. The titles bore witness to the musical emphasis of his outings. He rode into the dusty streets of about fifteen mythical towns, making shoot-'em-ups for Columbia,

performances with such acts as the popular Johnny Mercer and the Pied Pipers got Curtis back in the business. The real turning point came the day he first sang the western ballad "Tumblin' Tumbleweeds" over the air. Someone out there was paying attention; the next thing Curtis knew, he was signing a contract with Columbia Pictures.

In 1944 Curtis became Ken Curtis, according to his contract, and he was suddenly a singing cowboy, riding in the trails of such men

Ken Curtis as a Zorro-type character in the Republic serial *Don Daredevil Rides Again*. Phillips Archives.

Kayson/Screencraft, Lippert, and Republic. His melodious voice won him attention among fans of the subgenre.

After his B-western career tapped out, Curtis went on to character roles in various A-westerns, some directed by his father-in-law, the master western filmmaker John Ford. In 1956 Curtis appeared in the classic John Wayne movie *The Searchers*, playing the part of a Texas Ranger. He also made appearances in non-westerns and ventured into work behind the camera, producing such films as *The Killer Shrews*.

Moving to television, Curtis became a regular on a series called "Ripcord," portraying a skydiver. He also appeared in episodes of "Rawhide" and "Have Gun Will Travel" but is best remembered for his work as Festus on "Gunsmoke."

He began in "Gunsmoke" playing in various roles, starting with the December 8, 1962, episode "Us Haggens" and becoming a regular cast member with the January 18, 1964, episode "Prairie Wolfer." Eventually, he took over the role of deputy to Marshal Matt Dillon (James Arness), replacing Dennis Weaver's character Chester Goode with the unforgettable Festus

Ken Curtis as Festus Haggen with James Arness and Milburn Stone in the television series "Gunsmoke." Phillips Archives. Copyright CBS, Inc.

Haggen. Some longtime fans were so loyal to Weaver that they were reluctant to accept Curtis in the cast, but most were won over as soon as he had some time to prove his abilities.

Occasionally in "Gunsmoke" Curtis would burst into song, calling to mind his days as a singing cowboy star. Most often it was a hillbilly number or the calling of a square-dance tune, but in a few instances he sang something as serious as those he'd sung with the Sons of the Pioneers. On these occasions he

delivered a beautiful rendition, almost going against the image of Festus. Those performances were well worth capturing on tape.

Long after the demise of television's most popular and longest-running western, Ken Curtis could still be seen playing character roles in various western films like *The Shadow Riders*, based on a Louis L'Amour novel. His characters always added memorable moments to those pictures whose credits he graced. □

MONTE HALE

Although some sources have given his birthplace as Ada, Oklahoma, Monte Hale says he started out on June 8, 1921, in San Angelo, Texas. Raised there and around Sterling City, he learned to ride and rope as a youngster, although he admitted to falling off more than he stayed on. Despite his clumsiness in the saddle, he learned the guitar early on and was already considered a good singer by the age of twelve. He bought his first guitar for $8.50 in savings and started working barn dances, schoolhouses, rodeos—wherever folks would lend an ear.

In 1944 he ran into a bit of real luck while playing at the Jean Lafitte Hotel in Galveston, Texas. Entertainers were arriving by the

Hale and his horse, Pardner, strike a handsome balance in this Republic Pictures publicity still. Phillips Archives.

carload to do a War Bond drive called Stars Over Texas. Lee "Lasses" White, the cowboy sidekick of Jimmy Wakely, happened to be short a guitar picker, and Monte was able to land the job—not only for the evening's performance, but for the entire two weeks of the drive.

Among the entertainers were Chill Wills, Gail Storm, and Big Boy Williams. One of the stars was so impressed with Monte that he wrote to Herbert Yates of Republic Studios. Yates didn't promise anything but offered Monte the chance to meet some influential producers and directors if he would come out west.

Monte was so broke he couldn't even afford to go across town, but he located a friend in Houston who loaned him the money to get to

Monte Hale is about to get the drop on the bad guys in this still from Republic's *The Timber Trail*, 1948. Phillips Archives.

Monte Hale enjoyed a comic-book run by Fawcett/Charlton that saw fifty-nine issues between 1948 and 1956. Note the Thunderbird design boots that were already a trademark of Roy Rogers's by this time. Phillips Archives.

Hollywood. Upon meeting Yates, and with no previous acting experience—just his guitar and voice—Monte walked away with a seven-year contract.

As was customary, he played a number of supporting roles before getting a chance at a starring role. From his first outing, *Step in Society*, Monte appeared in eight films between 1944 and 1946, featuring such sagebrushers as Allan "Rocky" Lane, Richard Arlen, Wild Bill Elliott, and Sunset Carson.

Then, in 1946, it seemed that Monte's big moment had come. Thinking that their number-one cowboy, Roy Rogers, was about to be drafted, Republic assigned Monte to take Roy's place in *Don't Fence Me In*. Monte had already memorized all the lines when Roy's military deferment came through. The producers changed horses, understandably, and Roy continued his career while Monte hunted for another way onto the marquee as the headliner. He finally found it in

Republic's first color film, *Home on the Range*.

Riding those dusty movie trails on his horse Pardner, Monte came to be known as the easygoing cowboy, with a place all his own in the hearts of the theater-going public. He sang only occasionally in his nineteen B-western starring roles. Still, he possessed a fine singing voice and even dabbled in songwriting.

Color film was a perfect medium to show off Monte's good looks. The sartorial glitz of a wardrobe rivaling that of Roy Rogers, complete with shirts from the renowned custom tailors Nathan Turk and "Nudie" Cohen, is especially evident in the photos used for his string of comic books, one of the few commercial tie-ins with which Monte is associated. His comic book saw fifty-nine issues from October 1948 through January 1956. He also filled the covers and pages of *Western Hero* comics from 1949 to 1952, alongside cowboy greats like Hopalong

Cassidy and Tom Mix. It has been reported that Monte's comics collected sales of over two million copies per month, including sales in no fewer than twenty-seven different languages.

Unlike most of the prominent singing cowboys, Monte had a scanty recording career, with a few releases on Beltone and a couple on MGM Records in the late 1940s. There were also all kinds of tours: fairs, rodeos, theaters, and especially children's hospitals. In the fifties and sixties, Monte appeared on TV shows like "Juke Box Jury," "Gunsmoke," "Tales of Wells Fargo," and "Wild Bill Hickock."

Despite the great variety and quality of his work, Monte has always been known as the reluctant singing cowboy. He didn't look on himself as much of an actor and never really put his heart into making the pictures or into show business in general. Though he never showed it in public, he always felt that he really should have stayed at

home on the range. But his fans saw Hale as one cowboy who could just stop chasing the bad guys for a few minutes, lean up against a tree to sing a song, and still manage to catch the owlhoots. With the musical support of such groups as the Sons of the Pioneers and the Riders of the Purple Sage, Monte's films made for top-notch entertainment. He was even given a role in the classic 1955 film *Giant* after impressing the director with his ability to toss a cowboy hat on a rack. The great James Dean did a rope trick in one memorable scene, and Monte Hale taught it to him.

In recent years Monte has been in attendance at many of the nostalgic western-film festivals and enjoyed seeing old friends, fans, and other stars of yesteryear like his pal Gene Autry. He and his wife Joanne live near the southern California beaches and can often be seen tooling around Los Angeles with personalized plates that read "Texas 1." □

REX ALLEN

Rex Allen was the last of that special Hollywood breed to ride onto the silver screen, sitting tall in the saddle of a beautiful horse, strumming his guitar and singing a western ballad. Though he was the last singing cowboy to sign a film contract in Tinsel Town, he was also one of the "singingest" of the entire lot. It was an image Hollywood didn't have to invent; he came by it quite naturally.

Rex Allen was born in Willcox, Arizona, in 1921, and grew up on a ranch playing shoot-'em-up games in the mountains. At the age of ten, his

In keeping with a longstanding Hollywood tradition, Rex Allen's horse, Koko, was about as famous as his master. Phillips Archives.

The *Rodeo King and the Senorita* was released by Republic in 1951, actually a rewrite of John Wayne film *Cowboy and the Lady*. Phillips Archives.

Rex Allen and Koko in a publicity still for Republic Pictures. Rex was one of a few box-office buckaroos to wear his six-guns reversed in the holsters. Phillips Archives.

REX ALLEN
The Arizona Cowboy
KOKO
The Miracle Horse of the Movies

RODEO KING and the Senorita

with MARY ELLEN KAY
BUDDY EBSEN · ROY BARCROFT
Directed by Philip Ford · Written by John K. Butler

A REPUBLIC PICTURE

father, a popular country fiddler in the area, bought him his first guitar. The idea was to fashion Rex into a handy accompanist. Mastering the fine art of balladeering, he sang in glee clubs throughout his high school years and lent a rich voice to local church choirs.

Immediately after graduation, Rex landed a job at radio station KOY in Phoenix. Drawing on his ranch skills, he also tried his luck at professional rodeoing, work which carried him to Trenton, New Jersey. It was there, while getting the worst end of bouts with bulls and not making any real money, that Rex managed to croon his way into another singing job at Trenton station WTTM. Eventually he signed on with The Sleepy Hollow

DELL

SEPT.-NOV.
10¢

REX ALLEN

The fate of a town
depended on
**THE TREASURE OF
BLACK MOUNTAIN**

Rex Allen, late-arriving singing cowboy, made up for lost time when he came the closest to rivaling Roy Rogers's trademark attire . . . lots of fringe and flair. Rex's Dell comic series saw thirty-one issues from 1951 to 1959. Phillips Archives.

Gang, an Allentown, Pennsylvania, group that played in outdoor parks. Other performers suggested that Rex consider auditioning for Chicago's "National Barn Dance" on station WLS .

Rex headed straight for the Windy City in 1945 and made it onto the roster as a regular. He was popular enough with the audiences to win an emcee spot and got his own segment on the show. It was only natural that he would get movie offers from Hollywood. For a while he turned them down because of his lucrative income with WLS. According to an interview published in the late 1970s, Rex even turned down the chance to play a younger Hopalong Cassidy. As he made several friends who were doing well as singing cowboys in the musical westerns, including Gene Autry and Roy Rogers, the movie scene became more appealing to him. Herbert Yates, the big wheel at Republic, chanced to hear Rex on "Barn Dance" and made an offer he couldn't refuse. Rex flew to Holly-wood, passed his screen test, and signed on the dotted line. His first effort was the 1950 release entitled, appropriately enough, *The Arizona Cowboy*.

Phillips Petroleum, Rex's radio sponsor, moved his show out to California, where it was carried over CBS. Meanwhile, when Roy Rogers's contract with Republic expired and he moved to television, Rex took advantage of the space that opened up in the Republic corral, agreeing to keep his distance from television cameras.

He didn't get the benefit of the lavish budgets that Roy enjoyed, but he wasted no time establishing his own following. He rode in four to five western serials a year for Republic, with his mount, Koko, the "Miracle Horse of the Movies." Part Morgan, part quarter horse, sporting unusual markings, Koko was one of the most beautiful horses ever ridden across the silver screen and an animal extremely difficult to double.

Rex did everything by the numbers in the roles he played and in the life he bargained to have. His feature films numbered nineteen, made from 1950 to 1954. They are quite memorable for better-than-average story lines, action scenes directed by William Witney, attractive leading ladies such as Jeanne Cooper, and the wonderful sidekick Slim Pickens. Of course, there was also Rex's charming personality, not to mention his flashy attire: inlaid boots, snowy white hat, fringed shirts, and ornately tooled leather holsters and gun belt.

Rex toured all over the country in the rodeo circuit, singing and putting Koko through his paces. He also appeared in the Republic-produced television series "Frontier Doctor" (also known as "The Man of the West" and "Unarmed"), roaming the Arizona territory for thirty-nine episodes as Dr. Bill Baxter, armed with a medicine bag instead of a six-gun. The show was conceived by Rex, himself, just as he saw that television's popularity was about to grind the B-western to a halt.

Rex maintained a rewarding recording career on numerous labels from the 1940s through the 1960s, offering the public a unique voice with rich western accents. His selections on Decca, Vista, and Mercury covered authentic cowboy songs, country and western numbers, religious songs, and even novelty tunes. Among the really big hits for Allen were "Afraid" (1949), "Sparrow in the Treetop" (1951), "Marines, Let's Go" (1961), "Don't Go Near the Indians" (1962), "Crying in the Chapel" (1963), "Tear After Tear" (1964), and even "Tiny Bubbles" (1968).

Rex made numerous appearances on the big screen between 1960 and 1980. He also had a bit of luck just when he needed something new to ward off premature retirement: Walt Disney called and Rex wound up narrating nature films for over 150 episodes of Disney's "Wonderful World of Color" on NBC. He even became the voice for numerous cartoon characters, narrated the Hanna-Barbara animated feature "Charlotte's Webb," and became the subject of a series of Dell western comics that have become expensive collectibles in the 1990s. Rex could even be heard on television in the Purina Dog Chow commercials.

In 1982 Rex provided us with some beautifully delivered lines in the hit song made by his son Rex, Jr., "Last of the Silver Screen Cowboys." It was a fitting tribute to this man who wanted nothing more than to be noted and remembered for his delivery of a western song. □